DIM SUM

BY RHODA YEE

PUBLISHED BY TAYLOR & NG · SAN FRANCISCO · 1977

TO ALL DIM SUM LOVERS
IN THE WORLD-
THE JOY OF CHINESE COOKING
IS THAT YOU NEVER
WOK ALONE!

ISBN 0-912738-10-3
Library of Congress Card No. 77-89297
Printed in the United States of America
Copyright © 1977 Rhoda Yee
Published by Taylor & Ng
P.O. Box 200
Brisbane California 94005
    All Rights Reserved
    First Edition 3rd Printing
Distributed by Random House, Inc.
and in Canada by Random House of Canada, Ltd.
ISBN 0-394-73463-7

Photography by Alan Wood, Dennis Forbes, and Spaulding Taylor.

Designed by Win Ng and Alan Wood.

Taylor & Ng would like to give special thanks to the San Francisco Chinese Cultural Center for its loan of the rare musical instruments photographed on page 12.

ABOUT THE AUTHORESS

Rhoda Fong Yee was born in Canton, capital of Kwongtung province in Southern China. A good part of her childhood was spent in Loan Gon Doan, her father's village. It was her experience during this part of her childhood which inspired Rhoda to write *The Chinese Village Cookbook*, and now, *Dim Sum*.

At the age of twelve, Rhoda migrated to this country and settled in Sacramento, California. She learned the basics of Chinese cuisine from her mother, who is an excellent cook, having received training from several family chefs.

In 1962, three years after graduating from U.C. Berkeley, Rhoda married Paul Yee, who coincidentally shares her love and enthusiasm for Chinese food. Together, they have delighted their friends with scrumptious Chinese feasts in their home in Walnut Creek.

Rhoda began to give Chinese cooking instructions eight years ago. Her expertise in the Chinese culinary art, the vivaciousness of her personality and her quick sense of humor create an uncanny ability to establish fast rapport with her audiences. Besides carrying a full teaching schedule, Rhoda presents numerous Chinese cooking lectures and demonstrations throughout the U.S. and has participated in innumerable national and local television programs.

TABLE OF CONTENTS

PREFACE

I once read an article which said the favorite indoor sport of the Chinese people is cooking. Thank God it isn't something else, in view of the population of China!

Whoever made that statement is a very keen observer, for indeed, we are a race whose love of good eating transcends the rich, the poor, the young, the old, the scholarly and the illiterate. Nowhere will you find this passion more evident than in a local Chinese tea house where the famous *dim sum* lunches are served.

It is my intention in this book to take you on an armchair tour to a typical Chinatown tea house and to share with you some of my favorite tea-lunch dim sum recipes. In addition, to help you successfully present your own dim sum lunch, I have suggested menus for you to try. These are planned with the following two points in mind: (1) the food will be well balanced in taste and texture and (2) most of the dishes may be made ahead, so you will feel relaxed and able to enjoy your own party. Of course, the best part of all will be the compliments you'll receive!

I will also share with you amusing stories, daily customs and popular folklore I've heard and experienced in China, where I spent my childhood. I certainly hope this book will bring us a little closer to your hearts. After all, that's what "dim sum" means!

VISIT TO A TEA HOUSE

What Are "Dim Sums"?

What is a Chinese tea house? It is a Cantonese restaurant specializing in serving a particular kind of southern Chinese lunch which is called dim sum. Its literal translation is "dot heart." Poetically, it means "heart's delight"! And what an appropriate explanation, for dim sums are delicious tiny little bite-size morsels of stuffed savory meat or sweet dumplings—either deep-fried, baked or steamed, and served with a variety of tasty, hot or spicy dips. Dim sum can also be braised, marinated meats in aromatic and succulent sauces. For more substantial offerings, you can have noodles in soups with different garnishes or the more familiar pan-fried-style chowmein with different meats and vegetables. Another perennial favorite is *joak,* a thick rice soup usually served with a Chinese fried bread called Deep-Fried Devils.

The Meeting Place

How did Chinese tea houses get started? In every country, there usually is a type of gathering place (other than churches) where people congregate, companions meet and friends exchange pleasantries. In England, are the pubs, in France, bistros, and in America, the cocktail lounge, corner bar or the coffee house. In China, most people drink alcoholic beverages only on special occasions, so the familiar corner bar is non-existent. However, since tea is the favorite beverage in China, tea houses became popular. People used them as meeting places for both business and pleasurable family outings.

At first, there were no more than a dozen items on the menu but as more people frequented the tea houses, the demand for variety increased. Since the restaurant owners wanted to please their customers' insatiable appetites, more and more new and exotic items were invented and added to the menu, so that now it is not unusual to find restaurants offering 50 to 60 choices of dim sum each day!

In Hong Kong, many tea houses open as early as five o'clock in the morning, to accommodate the night-shift crowds. Of course, people who go to work in the morning usually stop there for a small bite of breakfast and read the morning papers or shoot the breeze with their fellow workers. The most hectic hours are from 11 o'clock in the morning to about two o'clock in the afternoon, when everybody fights their way in: the factory and office workers who grab quick meals, businessmen talking shop over a leisurely lunch, housewives between shopping errands, students on their lunch breaks, and coolies who welcome the respite from their daily toil. There are restaurants and roadside stands to suit every budget; no one brown bags.

If you've never been to a Chinese tea house, you should make it a point to visit one at the next available opportunity, because it is a most enjoyable experience that you will long remember. I've often taken my students on a Chinatown tour ending with a tea lunch, and it is always the highlight of the day. So come with me now and let me be your guide on our visit to a typical tea house.

Getting Yourself Ready

First of all, don't eat breakfast and plan on having the tea lunch as brunch. Get there by 11 in the morning and you'll have no trouble (most of the time) getting seated right away. Any later and you may have to wait for a whole hour, especially on weekends. It is more advantageous for you to get together a group of friends numbering eight to ten so that you may be able to taste a greater variety of dim sum. Order each type of dish for sampling so that you will be able to try a good number of available items. Be sure to bring paper and pen to jot down the names and descriptions of each dish you try and star the ones you like. On ensuing visits, try something different; soon, you'll have sampled everything!

The Proper Atmosphere

Upon entering a tea house, your first impression is one of complete chaos and confusion! You'll hear voices in both Chinese and English and, more often than not, kids squealing and crying at the same time. Dishes and tea cups clatter noisily as waiters clean up tables. Waitresses, while pushing tea carts loaded with all kinds of dim sum, call out loudly in Chinese in a sing-song manner the names of each goodie as they pass by the tables. Adding to the din, you may even see what appears to be a hotly contested argument at one of the tables, the participants looking as though they're almost at fist blows, grabbing and shuffling. You are about to call the manager, but wait! The fighting just stopped and everyone is smiling and shaking hands! What gives? Actually, they are trying to pay for the lunch and all that "physical violence" is to determine who can grab the bill!

You see, it is Chinese custom to insist on paying for the meal when you are dining with a friend. There is no such thing as Dutch treat. Even if you know in advance that you are being treated, you must go through the motion of insisting on paying as a courtesy to your host. The moral of the story is, don't ask just anybody you bump into to join you for lunch, unless you're willing to accept the chances of your footing the bill for the other person.

But don't let all the noise and confusion prejudice you in any way because, believe it or not, this is the typical atmosphere of the tea house and many Chinese restaurants in general. I judge the restaurant not so much by its décor (afterall, how much décor can you eat?), but I look for places where I can get good food without having to pay through the nose. I've been to restaurants where the décor is beautiful, lights are dim, waiters are in dinner jackets and people speak in whispers. Such atmosphere in a Chinese restaurant is totally lacking in ethnic character. I want a place with a minimum of frills, (some of the best eating places have bare walls and very very sparse furniture), where the help is clean but less formally attired, the dining room fairly well lighted (I want to see what I'm eating!), with a healthy number of Chinese families in attendance. I love to hear the clanging of Chinese cooking utensils, the sizzling noise of food cooking in woks and the rhythmic pounding of cleavers coming from the kitchen. Can't you just visualize the chef creating with his heart and soul dish after delicious dish for his loyal subjects who wait with tongues hanging and mouths salivating? Oh! This is music to my ears! Don't fight it! Enjoy it and become part of the happy confusion!

Tea-Lunch Etiquette

After you've survived the initial shock and are seated, the first thing is to select your tea. This is the only time you have a choice of tea, because at dinner time only one kind of tea is served to all dinners. But, since this is a tea lunch, you have the fun of deciding. (The only exception I've found so far are Chinese tea houses in Honolulu, where they serve you the "house tea" of their choice.) As a starter, jasmine or lichee are very good teas, as they are light and highly fragrant. Some other teas you may try are *kuan yin,* dragon well (*loan jang*) or *po nay,* a tea we nick-named the "Chinese Alka-Selzer" because of its ability to cut through grease (if the food is too oily) and, at the same time, soothe your tummy. Should you need to have your tea pot refilled during the course of your meal, just flip the cover upside down and instantly (well, most of the time) your waiter or waitress will appear like magic to give you a fresh pot of tea!

Don't look for a menu because there usually is none if yours is a typical tea house. The food is usually brought from the kitchen on a tea cart or hand carried on a tray. When the food passes by you, wave the waitress over (sometimes you have to shout to get her attention) and take whatever looks good to you. If you don't know what they are, the waitress will usually explain.

Even though you may be hungry (STARVED is more like it for me), don't be in a hurry to order everything from the first cart that comes along (How about leaving the cart here with me, lady?) or you'll fill yourself up too quickly (God gave me two ears to hear, why only one mouth to eat?) and not able to try more dim sum later on. (You wanna bet? Those Hawaiian muu muus can hide a multitude of sins, or in this case, just one big fat lump!) The idea of a tea lunch is: 1) to enjoy each morsel at a leisurely pace; 2) sip the tea slowly (It is important that you purse your lips and suck in a little air while sipping, enabling you to cool the hot tea as you drink it; if you happen to create a slight slurping sound, you've got it! Emily Post would blush for you, but Confucious would nod with approval!); 3) wait for your next favorite things to come by. No one will be in a hurry to remove you, so take your time and enjoy! (In this case, do as I say, not as I do—unless you've brought your own muu muu.)

If you wish to have a noodle dish, such as chowmein or *lo mein,* you must place the order with the waitress because these are specially cooked to order.

At the end of the lunch, the waitress merely counts up the number of dishes you have on the table (tea-lunch restaurants charge by the dish) and then tabulates the cost of the meal. When I was still going to school, my friend and I, on a dare, hid the little dishes from the waiter when time came for him to add up our bill. Of course it was a stupid thing to do, for, had we been caught, we would have ended up washing dishes in the kitchen all day or, worst yet, in jail! My father told me that when he was a student in Hong Kong, they were even more daring. They used to throw the dishes out of the window as soon as they finished eating the food! So the next time you walk by a Chinese restaurant and see a dish come sailing by . . .!

THE ANCIENT WOK IN THE MODERN KITCHEN

Before we get into dim sum recipes, I think it would be appropriate to first discuss the various equipment you may need, such as a wok, cleavers, steamers and/or steam racks, etc. Knowing how to use these tools and having them at your disposal will help you tremendously and give you a great deal more pleasure in cooking Chinese foods.

The Wok And Its Accessories

This bowl-shaped vessel with a dome-shaped cover is used for stir-frying, deep-frying and steaming. Because of its unique shape, you will find less oil is needed for stir-frying as well as deep-frying. In steaming, its dome-shape allows condensed steam to travel down the side of the cover, thus preventing excess condensation dropping directly from the top as with flat-topped covers.

In my *Chinese Village Cookbook*, I go to great lengths on buying, seasoning, usage and caring of the wok and its accessories, such as the stir-fry ladle, spatula, bamboo-handled wire strainers, chopsticks and cleavers. This is all equipment which you should have to truly master the art of dim sum. I suggest you refer to that particular chapter in the book for complete information on those subjects. Besides, the *Chinese Village Cookbook* is full of mouth-watering Cantonese recipes I know you'll love and treasure!

STEAMING

This is a process in which food is cooked by the steam of boiling water. Food cooked this way, be it vegetables, fish, fowl or other types of meats, needs no additional oil because it is cooked slowly in its own natural juices. The food is moist, tender and retains more nutrients than left after other cooking methods. Those of you who have tried my Steamed Fish or Steamed Chicken in the *Chinese Village Cookbook* know what I'm talking about. (My mouth waters just thinking about these dishes!) It is indeed a very healthy and popular method of Chinese cooking, and you'll find it often applied in dim sum recipes.

There are many kinds of steamers and steaming accessories available. Let's go through them one by one.

Steaming Racks There are numerous steaming racks to choose from. One consists of two wooden sticks, each with a notch cut in the middle so they fit to form a cross. It is placed over boiling water in a wok to serve as a platform for any heat-proof dish. A cover is placed over the wok to contain the steam.

A second type is a stainless-steel rack shaped like the tic-tac-toe sign. This fits into the wok just like the wooden steam rack and is used the same way. It's collapsible for storage.

A third rack, and I think the best available, is a round steam rack shaped like a wagon wheel. It is made of light-weight chrome and is used in the same manner as the other racks. The design provides a steady surface for the bowl or dish to rest on and allows maximum clearance for steam circulation. It can also double as a countertop trivit!

Bamboo Steamer This is a tiered steamer that sits over boiling water in a wok. The bottom of each tier is much like lattice work and allows steam to circulate around the food placed on each layer. A lid over the top contains the steam. The food can be placed directly on the lattice work layers, as when steaming Pork Buns. Or food can be placed first in a heat-proof dish and then set on the steamer rack, as when making steamed fish or steamed pork. Since steamers come in tiers, several different foods can be cooked concurrently, saving time, fuel and space. Avoid storing steamers in dry, hot places since the bamboo will buckle and break around the seams. When not in use, they make unique fruit bowls or they can become flower pots by placing a shallow dish with floral arrangements inside.

3 Layer Aluminum Steamer So far, I've discussed steamer and steaming accessories which require the use of the wok. Now, here's one that will function all on its own! This 10 inch or 12 inch diameter aluminum steamer with a dome shaped cover comes with a bottom pot and two steam tiers, one resting on top of the other. The cooking principle is the same as for the bamboo steamer, only now the bottom pot holds the boiling water—no wok is necessary. (This bottom pot can also double as a pasta cooker for such things as noodles, wonton, etc.) You can store this light weight steamer easily and compactly by nesting the bottom pot into one of the steamer tiers and then setting the other steamer on top. The dome shaped cover is turned upside down and nests perfectly into the steamer to further shorten the height of the entire set.

If you only have one wok at home and you need it for other stir fry dishes, this aluminum steamer is the answer to your prayers!

PORTABLE BURNER BY TAYLOR & NG

This denatured alcohol burner has a removable top which doubles as a steam rack when placed inside a wok. When left on, it can accommodate various sizes of skillets and crepe or omelet pans for cooking. Once removed, the opening fits either a 12 or 14 inch wok.

The heat coming from the burner is very hot, comparable to the heat one gets on the big burner at home. Therefore, it is an excellent second heat source for wok cooking, especially if you have someone else who likes to cook Chinese food and you find your range is a bit cramped for two people to work elbow to elbow. This way, the second person can stir fry anywhere in the kitchen.

The portable burner is also good for camping and backyard cookouts. It is a great warmer for your buffet table; the heat is adjustable. Should your electricity ever get shut off in an emergency and you are in the midst of cooking, have no fear, as long as you have this little portable burner and a bottle of denatured alcohol on hand.

PASTA MACHINE (OR NOODLE MAKER)

If you are one who enjoys making your own noodles, you will find a noodle making machine a joy to use. It has detachable parts so you can vary the noodle width. You can also make thin sheets of noodles for egg rolls or wonton skins. Do not wash the parts after use. Just let it dry and brush off the excess flour and dry dough. Invest in a heavy and substantial noodle maker instead of a light weight machine, because the latter kind will wobble and move all over the place when you are rolling out the dough.

TORTILLA PRESS (METAL)

It is excellent for pressing out dough to the desired size and thickness for certain dim sum items such as Shrimp Bonnets (*Ha Gow*), Steamed Pork Turnovers (*Fun Gor*), Pot Stickers (*Kuo Teh*), Onion Pancakes, Peking Doilies, etc. It is not at all expensive and it will save you hours of rolling out dough by hand.

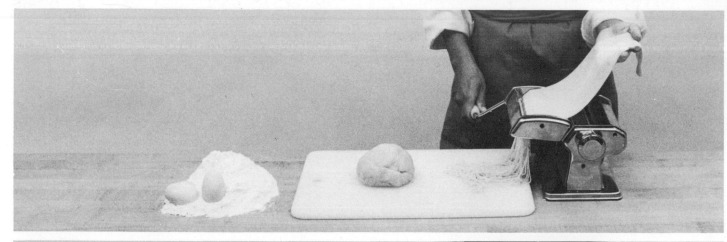

THE FIVE CLASSIC WRAPS

The majority of dim sum specialties are wrapped in dough of some sort and there are many more than the following five. But these five are the most common and basic, for in them, you'll find a great variety of fillings. Consequently, many of the classic dim sum recipes evolve from just these basic wrappers.

For your convenience, I am presenting these five recipes in 1 section for quick reference. Whenever you come across a recipe requiring one of the basic five, it will be so indicated, and all you have to do is to turn to these few pages for the appropriate recipe. This small but very important section will give you, at a glance, a quick comparison of the differences in ingredients used, techniques employed and cooking methods required for these wrappers. Once you master the techniques for making these five types of wrappers, you'll be well on your way to becoming a good dim sum chef!

Steamed or Baked Bun Dough

Yield: 2 doz buns

1 cake of fresh compressed yeast
1¾ cup warm water
¾ cup sugar
1 tsp baking powder
6½ cups unsifted all purpose flour

To Make Dough: Dissolve ½ yeast cake with sugar in warm water. Immediately add baking powder and then the flour. The dough will be fairly firm and a bit on the dry side. Knead on board for 20 minutes (you should not need to flour the board) until dough becomes elastic and smooth. Place it in a big mixing bowl, cover with a damp cloth and leave in a dry, warm place (away from drafts) until dough doubles in bulk. (Every kitchen is different. My dough usually takes about 2½ to 3 hours to double in my electric oven, which I slightly preheat to a warm setting for 2-3 minutes then turn off.) Now punch down dough and knead again for 5 more minutes. It is now ready to be stuffed with fillings.

Comments: This is just a basic yeast dough with perhaps a bit more sugar added. For those of you who do not care to make this from scratch, you may use frozen bread dough as a substitute.

Egg Noodle Dough

Yield: 1½ lb egg noodles

or
80 to 100 sheets wonton wrappers (3 to 3½ inch sq) or 25 sheets egg roll wrappers (5 to 5½ inch sq)

3 extra large eggs
2⅔ tbsp water
3 cups unsifted all purpose flour

To make dough by hand: Beat eggs with water, then add flour. Beat in the first 2 cups in your mixer and the last cup by hand, as the dough is very dry. Mix until the ingredients adhere. Knead on board (no need to flour the board) for at least 10-15 minutes, until dough is smooth. Divide dough into 2 balls keeping one covered while you work with the other.

Roll out to desired thinness then cut into narrow strips for noodles or the appropriate squares for wonton skins or egg roll wrappers. (These should be as thin as possible.)

To make dough by machine: Mix and knead dough as described above. Roll dough by hand so it is thin enough to fit through the widest slot of the kneading section of the noodlemaker. Run it through once. Then continue to run dough through the slot, but increasing the thinness gauge until you have the dough at the desired width. The dough is now ready for any 1 of the following steps.

Fresh Egg Noodles: Put on the egg noodle attachment and run dough once through the egg noodle slot. Cut noodles to desired length. Dust with cornstarch. Wrap in plastic wrap and place in refrigerator.

Wonton Wrappers: Run dough twice through the last or next to the last slot. (The dough should be as thin as possible.) Cut dough into 3 or 3½ inch squares. Dust with cornstarch and stack wrappers on top of each other. Wrap in plastic wrap and store in refrigerator.

Egg Roll Wrappers: Run dough twice through the same slot just like the wonton wrappers. Cut into 5 or 5½ inch squares. The size of the square is determined by the width of the dough. Therefore, try to keep the width of the rolled out sheet to almost, or as wide as, the width of the noodle slot. The minimum width should be at least 5 inches but is even better if it is 5½ inches.

Do ahead notes: Noodles or wrappers can keep in the refrigerator for several days or in the freezer for several weeks.

Comments: It is much easier and more fun if you use the noodle maker machine, especially in making wonton and egg roll wrappers. It is very difficult, if not impossible, to hand roll the dough out as thin as the machine can. Home made noodles and wrappers are so much better than store bought ones (they are available in most oriental food stores and supermarkets) that, once you've made them, you're hooked!

It's a fun family project because your children will love seeing the noodles and wrappers being rolled out by the little machine. They'll fight to get their turn to help crank the slot, help feed the dough through, or cut and dust the wrappers. I recommend doubling or tripling the recipe so you'll have enough to use for several weeks, since they freeze so well.

Rice Noodle Dough (Fun)

Yield: 1 doz noodle rolls

> 2 cups Swansdown cake flour (no substitute)
> ¼ cup wheatstarch (or cornstarch)
>
> 1 tsp salt
> ⅓ cup oil
> 2⅔ cups cold water

To make dough: Mix above in order given. Make sure the batter is smooth and free of lumps. Ladle ⅓ cup into an oiled 9 inch pie pan. Steam for 5 minutes. Cool. Roll up jelly roll style. Wipe pie pan clean, oil again and repeat procedure until all the batter is used. The steamed dough is now ready for stir fry or to be stuffed with fillings.

Do-ahead notes: These can be made ahead and kept at room temperature for 24 hours. The storage depends entirely on individual recipes utilizing this dough.

Comments: To facilitate the cooking, use 2 pie pans; one can be cooking while the other one is cooling off. You will find that it may be necessary to wash the pans between steaming. Be sure to wipe pans completely dry and re-oil each time or the batter will not roll off as easily.

Rice noodles can be purchased in stores in Chinatown but are not usually available in supermarkets. That's why it is necessary to learn to make them yourself. Besides, they're so good, I guarantee you'll be making them often.

Wheat Starch Dough

Yield: 3-4 doz wrappers

> 1 cup wheat starch
> ⅔ cup tapioca starch
> ½ tsp salt
> 2 tsp oil
> 1 cup & 2 tbsp boiling water

To make dough: Mix well the first 4 ingredients in order given. Bring water to a rolling boil and stir into dry ingredients with chopsticks until dry ingredients adhere. Cover and let it cool for 15 minutes. Lightly oil kneading surface and knead dough for several minutes, until dough is well mixed and smooth. Now it is ready for wrapping.

Do-ahead notes: Dough can be kept at room temperature for 1 day if you wrap it in plastic wrap. But I usually have fillings ready for wrapping right away.

Comments: It is very important that the water for the dough be boiling vigorously for several minutes before mixing with the starches. One sure way to have just the right amount of water is by first having a larger quantity than is called for in the recipe. Bring water to a rolling boil for 5 minutes then measure off the proper amount, return the water to the emptied pot, bring it to a vigorous boil again, adding to starch mixture *right away*. If the water is cooled off even for just a few seconds, the starch will not get cooked and the dough will fall apart. (You'll see the dough taking on a chalky white appearance instead of a transparent look. This indicates it is properly cooked.)

To insure dough is rolled evenly, a tortilla press will work wonders! (See recipes for Ha Gow and Steamed Pork Turnovers).

Glutinous Rice Dough

Yield: 2½ to 3 doz wrappers

> **Salty dough:**
> 2¼ cups glutinous-rice flour
> ¼ cup potato flour
> ¾ tsp salt
> ½ tsp sugar
> 1½ cup boiling water

To make wrapper: Bring a pot of water to a rolling boil for several minutes. Meanwhile, combine the first 4 ingredients. Now, measure the amount of water needed and return that to a boil and immediately pour the boiling water over the dry ingredients. Mix well and knead on floured board for 3 or 4 minutes.

> **Sweet dough:**
> 2 cups glutinous rice flour
> 1½ mashed, cooked sweet potato (1¼ lb)
> 1 cup brown sugar (lightly packed)
> ¼ cup water

To make wrapper: Mix the first 2 ingredients in a bowl. Dissolve brown sugar in water and bring to a rolling boil. Immediately add water to flour mixture and stir until dough is firm. Knead lightly for a few minutes until dough is well mixed.

Comments: This dough is usually deep fried with meat or sweet fillings. The texture is most interesting because the wrappers become soft and chewy on the inside and crunchy and crispy on the outside.

THE THREE "B'S" OF DIM SUM

The three great composers, Bach, Beethovan and Brahms, sometimes known as the three "Bs," were giants in the classical era. Their works have been well known and much loved through the centuries. They dominated the music of their times and had an indelible influence on much of the music composed in the decades following the classical era.

So what do Bach, Beethovan and Brahms have in common with dim sum in this chapter? Permit me to explain, if I may be so bold and presumptuous, that in the world of dim sum, there are many delectable items which are long time favorites. These are considered the "classics" of dim sum. They were forerunners to all the others.

Marco Polo's Favorite

Take the wonton, for instance. My grandmother used to tell me this story with great national pride. These meat and shrimp filled dumplings in thin egg noodle wrappers date as far back as the 13th century when Marco Polo made his visit to China. He was so fond of the wonton and noodles that he took samples back to Italy. And, you guessed it, that was the beginning of ravioli and spaghetti!

甜酸炸雲呑 **Fried Wonton
with Sweet and Sour Sauce Dip**

Yield: About 60-70 wonton

1 lb home made wonton skins *(see page 10)*
½ lb fresh ground pork
½ lb fresh prawns
4 dried mushrooms, soaked for 2 hours
8 water chestnuts, finely chopped
2 stalks green onions, finely chopped
2 small eggs, beaten
¼ tsp pepper
1½ tsp salt

Preparation: Shell and devein prawns. Finely mince. Stem mushrooms and mince caps. Mix with prawns, pork, water chestnuts, green onions, half of the beaten eggs and all of the seasonings.

Wrapping: Place wonton squares on working surface so corners face up, down, left and right. Place 1 tsp. filling in the center of each skin. Dip a little of the beaten egg on the bottom corner, bring top corner to meet bottom corner. Press to seal. Moisten left corner and bring right corner to meet it. Press to seal.

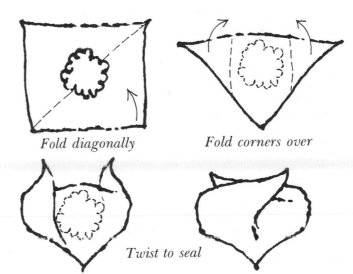

Fold diagonally *Fold corners over*

Twist to seal

Frying: Heat 4 cups oil in wok. Fry wrapped wonton until golden (about 2 min.) and turn over once. Drain and serve hot.

Do-ahead notes: Deep fry wonton, cool and freeze. To reheat, preheat oven at 350°. Place frozen wonton onto cookie sheet and heat for 12-15 min.

Sweet and Sour Sauce Dip

Yield: About 3 cups

½ cup brown sugar
1 tsp salt
½ cup vinegar
1½ tbsp cornstarch
4 tsp catsup
¾ cup pineapple juice
1 cup crushed pineapple

Cooking: Mix cornstarch and pineapple juice in a sauce pan. Add remaining ingredients. Stir over medium-high heat until sauce thickens. Add more liquid if sauce needs thinning or more cornstarch if you want sauce thicker. You can use additional juice or vinegar depending on how sour you want the sauce to be.

Do-ahead notes: Make sauce, cool, place in glass jar, freeze. To reheat, thaw and reheat in small sauce pan.

Comments: You may substitute ground turkey for pork in the wonton filling. However, since turkey is drier and more bland than pork, add a few more water chestnuts and ¼ tsp. monosodium glutamate to enhance flavor and texture.

14

The Drunken Chef

No one is quite sure of the origin of the Shrimp Bonnet (*Ha Gow*), but according to my 80 year old aunt, she was told that it came about quite by accident long ago. The story is that one of the chefs in the royal household of China came to work roaring drunk. He proceeded to make what was called the shrimp dumpling at that time; but, instead of using rice flour, he made the mistake of making the dough with wheat starch so that when steamed, the wrapper became transparant and the color of the cooked shrimp filling showed through in a most-delicate pink. The emperor was delighted with the chef's ingenuity and immediately rewarded him handsomely. The chef was so drunk it took him several days before he realized his beautiful and lucrative mistake!

Shrimp Bonnet (Ha Gow)

Yield: 4 doz

Dough:
1 recipe of the wheat starch dough *(pg.11)*

Filling:
¾ lb. prawns: cleaned, shelled & minced
¾ cup minced bamboo shoots
½ cup minced, cooked pork fat
1 stalk minced green onions
2½ tbsp cornstarch
1 tsp sesame oil
1 tsp oil
1 tsp light soy sauce
3 pinches white pepper
4 tsp sugar
½ tsp salt

Fried Wonton

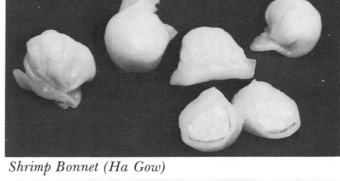

Shrimp Bonnet (Ha Gow)

Steamed Meat Dumplings (Siu Mai)

Spring Rolls (Chun Guen)

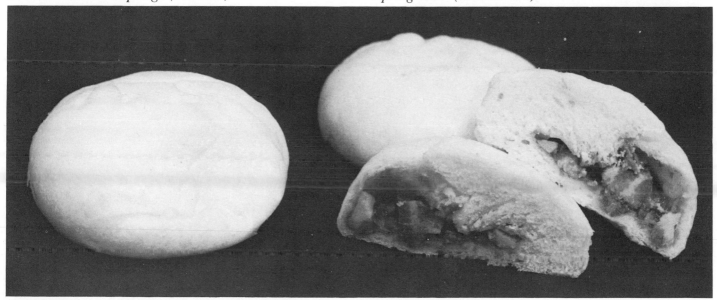

Steamed Barbecued Pork Buns (Cha Siu Bow)

To make filling: Combine above ingredients and chill for several hours (for ease of handling) before wrapping.

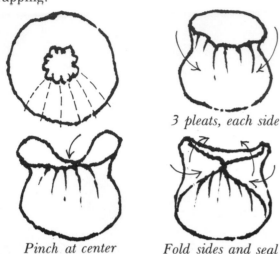

3 pleats, each side

Pinch at center   *Fold sides and seal*

Wrapping: Divide dough into 4 parts. Roll each part into a ½ inch wide sausage like strip. Cut strip into ¾ inch lengths (about 12 segments). Roll out each segment into approximately 3 inch to 3½ inch rounds. Pick out a point of reference anywhere on the edge of the circle. Make 3 pleats on each side toward the point. This will form a pouch. Place 1 tsp. filling into the opening, then press to seal just at the center part. Make one more pleat on each side (still pleating toward the center) then press remainder of opening to seal, gently shaping with fingers to give the shrimp bonnet a slightly curved appearance.

Steaming: Oil cake or pie pan and lay bonnets single layer, pleated side up. Steam for 15 minutes. Let cool for 2-3 minutes before handling. Serve with light soy sauce for dip. If you are using a bamboo or aluminum steamer, place cheese cloth on the steam rack before laying out the bonnets. This will prevent the bonnets from sticking.

Do ahead notes: The cooked bonnets can be kept for several days in the refrigerator or 2-3 weeks in the freezer. In either case, keep them well wrapped to prevent discoloration. Reheat by steaming, 10 minutes from refrigerator or 20 minutes from freezer.

Comments: It is definitely an advantage if you have a tortilla press to flatten the dough rather than rolling it by hand. In using the tortilla press, first roll each of the cut dough pieces into a round ball by hand, place in press and press. The dough will automatically flatten into the proper size and thickness. Remember, the thinner the dough, the prettier the bonnet. You'll be thrilled at the result, both in appearance and taste!

I'll bet you that the same son of a gun who invented the last recipe invented this next one too, considering how well his other mistake turned out.

Steamed Pork Turnovers (Fun Guaw)

Yield: 3 doz

Dough:
　　1 recipe of the wheat starch dough *(pg. 11)*

Filling:
　　1 lb minced fresh pork butt
　　12 water chestnuts
　　1 tbsp minced salted turnips *(choan choy)*
　　4 dried mushrooms
　　1 tbsp sugar
　　¾ tsp salt
　　¼ tsp white pepper
　　1 stalk minced green onion

Sauce mixture:
　　1 tbsp cornstarch
　　2 tsp light soy sauce
　　2 tbsp sherry
　　1 tbsp sugar

　　2 tsp oil

To make filling: Soak dried mushrooms for 1 hour or until soft. Discard stems and mince cap finely. Mix sauce. In wok or skillet, heat 2 tsp. oil, stir-fry pork, water chestnuts, salted turnips and mushrooms, add seasonings, then sauce mixture, and stir to mix well. (Sauce mixture is very thick.) Add green onions last. Chill thoroughly (for ease of handling) before wrapping.

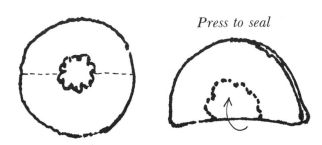

Press to seal

Wrapping: Divide dough into 3 parts. Roll each part into ¾ inch wide sausage like strips. Cut each strip into ¾ inch wide segments. Roll each segment into 4 inch rounds. Place 1 tbsp. (or more) filling on center, bring opposite sides together and pinch to seal.

Steaming: Same as for Shrimp Bonnets. (See preceeding recipe.) You can lay the turnovers on their sides or have them stand up with the seams facing upward.

Do-ahead notes: Same as Shrimp Bonnets. (See preceeding recipe.)

It was a common sight in many parts of China, more so in the cities than in the countryside, to see vendors selling ready to eat dim sum and noodle dishes. The steamed meat dumpling (*siu mai*) is one such dim sum item found at road side stands or in the most expensive tea houses. It is truly one of the all time favorites among the Chinese people.

Steamed Meat Dumplings (Siu Mai)

燒賣

Yield: About 10 doz

> 1 lb ground pork sausage
> 1 lb fresh ground pork
> 2 tsp salt
> 15 water chestnuts, finely chopped
> 1-2 tbsp minced fresh ginger
> ½ cup cornstarch
> ½ cup chicken broth
> 1 tbsp light soy sauce
> 1 tbsp salted turnips *(choan choy)*, finely minced
> 4 tbsp sugar
> 1 tsp terriyaki sauce
> 1 tsp sherry
> 1 tsp seasame oil
> ½ cup Chinese parsley, finely chopped
> 1 stalked green onions, finely chopped
> 1 pkg wonton skins
>   *or*
> 1 recipe of egg noodle dough *(pg. 9)*

Preparation: Mix all ingredients except wonton skins.

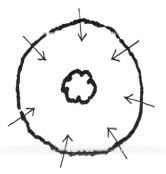

Press gathers to seal

Gather edge to enclose filling

Wrapping: Trim off 4 corners of wonton skins to form circles. Drop 1 tsp. mixture onto middle of the skin, gather up skin sides, letting the dough pleat naturally.

Flatten top and give the middle a light squeeze while tapping the bottom on a flat surface so it will stand upright.

Steaming: Arrange dumplings in an 8 inch round cake pan. Set pan on the steam rack in the wok. Fill bottom of wok with water. Cover. Steam for 15-20 minutes. Serve hot with a sesame oil and soy sauce dip. (1 part sesame oil to 2 parts light soy sauce.)

Do ahead notes: Steam dumplings. Cool and freeze. Reheat by steaming again for 12-15 minutes.

Comments: Insert toothpicks for easy serving. If you use a bamboo or aluminum steamer, place dumplings directly on the rack without the cake pan. Steam for the same amount of time.

Since steam dumplings can be made ahead and reheated in great quantities they make marvelous hors d'oeuvres for large cocktail parties. The two-tier aluminum steamer works particularly well.

The Three Headed Monster

There once lived a three-headed monster in the West River of southern China. He was a very evil monster (are there any nice ones?) and he ruled the entire river. Everytime a boat passed, the passengers had to make a sacrifice by throwing a human head (what a terrible diet!) into the river to insure safe passage. Otherwise the monster would cause the water in the river to churn so violently the boat would overturn and everyone would drown.

One day, a hot and lazy Sunday morning, a boat load of passengers was slowly cruising down the river. The captain announced that it was time for passengers to draw straws to see who would end up being Sunday brunch.

Now, as luck would have it, the man who drew the short end of the straw was Foo Yu, an artist, court jester and, generally, a man of varied talents. Needless to say, he was not overly enthusiastic with this stupid idea. So he quickly bribed the chef to make a big batch of bread dough stuffed with lots of meats and vegetables. Foo Yu adroitly shaped the filled dough into a human head and, with his brushes, painted on his face in no time flat. The chef brought the filled bun to top side and threw it overboard in front of the unsuspecting boat passengers. The boat passed by the three headed monster without incident and that was the cheery beginning of steamed barbecued pork buns! (Score another one for home cooking!)

Steamed Barbecued Pork Buns (Cha Siu Bow)

义燒包

Yield: 2 doz

Dough: 1 recipe of bun dough *(page 9)*

Filling:
    4 cups finely diced barbecued pork *(page 26)*
    ½ cup dehydrated onion flakes

Sauce mixture:
    2 tsp *hoisin* sauce
    2 tsp sherry
    4 tsp oyster sauce
    2 tsp catsup
    1 tsp sugar
    1½ tbsp cornstarch
    1½ cup chicken stock

To make filling: Soak onion flakes in a cup with just enough water to cover flakes. Mix sauce in a small sauce pan. Cook over medium high heat until sauce thickens. Stir in the diced pork and onion flakes. Chill 3-4 hours.

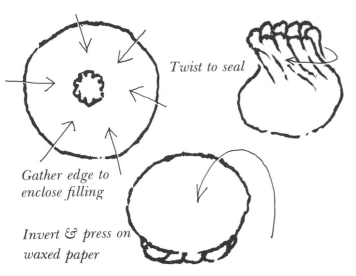

Twist to seal

Gather edge to enclose filling

Invert & press on waxed paper

Wrapping: Divide filling into 24 portions. Divide dough into 24 balls. Slightly flatten each ball then roll out into 4-inch discs, leaving the center of the disc twice as thick as the side. Place 1 portion of the filling in the center of the dough. Gather up the sides around the filling and twist dough to seal. Place on a 2 inch square piece of wax paper, twist side down. Put the wrapped buns at least 2 inches apart on a cookie sheet and allow the buns to rise in a draft-free place (the oven) for another hour.

Steaming: Steam for 15 minutes. Turn heat off and let the steam subside before lifting the cover.

Baking: *Cha Siu Bow* can also be baked. Preheat oven at 350°. Set buns 2 inches apart on cookie sheet. Brush with a mixture of 1 beaten egg white, 1 tsp. water and ¼ tsp. sugar. Bake for 20-25 minutes or until golden brown. Brush with melted butter.

Do ahead notes: Cook and freeze. Reheat by steaming if steam-cooked originally. Steam frozen buns for ½ hour to reheat. If baked, thaw and wrap buns in foil or cover pan with foil and reheat in slow oven for ½ hour.

Comments: A good filling should have some pork fat mixed in with the lean meat. Most importantly, *Cha Siu Bow* filling should be very juicy. That's why I use so much liquid in the sauce mixture. By chilling the

filling thoroughly, the sauce, which is very thick, adheres to the filling much better. Ideally, when you make the barbecued pork, you should try to save the pork drippings and use them as part of the sauce mixture.

I deliberately leave the center of the dough a bit thick because, if you roll it out to an even thickness, the top of the bun will ended up being too thin in comparison to the bottom due to of the way the dough is wrapped.

In a pinch, you may use frozen bread dough as a substitute. However, frozen dough works best when baked. It does not steam well.

Spring Rolls (Chun Guen)

Yield: 24

1 package of egg roll or spring-roll skins
   or
1 recipe of the egg noodle dough *(pg. 9)*
2 cups cooked ham or barbecued pork
5 medium sized dried mushrooms
1 cup bamboo shoots
1 cup shredded *napa* cabbage
½ lb fresh bean sprouts
3 stalks celery
2 stalks green onions

Sauce mixture:
   1 tsp salt
   2 tsp sugar
   2 tbsp oyster sauce
   2 tsp cornstarch
   ¼ cup chicken broth
4 cups oil for deep frying
1 egg, beaten

Preparation: Soak mushrooms until soft, discard stems. Slice ham, mushrooms, bamboo shoots and onions to the size of a match stick. On the diagonal, slice celery into strips of the same size. Rinse bean sprouts in cold water. Drain well. Mix sauce.

Filling: Heat wok, add 1 tbsp. oil. Stir fry separately and set aside: bean sprouts, 1 min.; celery, 2 min.; mushrooms with bamboo shoots, 2 min.; *napa* cabbage, 2 minutes; ham, 2 min. Add more oil as needed. Pour sauce mixture over ham and mix until sauce thickens. (Sauce will be very thick.) Return other ingredients plus the green onions and mix well. Cool before wrapping.

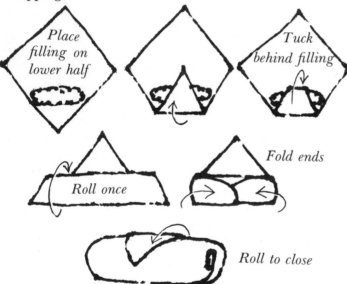

Wrapping: Position wrapper like a diamond with the corners at top, bottom, left and right. Place about ⅓ cup of filling on lower section of wrapper. Tuck bottom corner around filling and roll *firmly* about half way up the sheet. Moisten the remaining 3 corners with beaten egg. Fold left and right corners toward the center and roll all the way up.

Frying: Heat oil in wok. Deep fry Spring Rolls on both sides until golden brown, turning once. Drain on paper towels. Serve hot.

Do ahead notes: Fry Spring Rolls. Cool. Just before serving, deep fry again.

Comments: Cut Spring Rolls with kitchen scissors. Fresh pork butt, prawns or chicken also may be used. If you're a vegetarian, you can do away with the meat entirely. Instead, add shredded red and/or green pepper, snow peas, etc.

Spring Rolls are served during Chinese New Year to visiting friends and relatives; and, since the New Year usually falls around February, these tasty deep fried meat and vegetable rolls became known as Spring Rolls. The name "egg roll" derived from dipping the wrapped rolls in an egg batter before deep frying. The traditional Chinese method is without batter.

Wheat is the basic starch of the northern Chinese; rice, the basic starch of southern China. However, we are all very fond of noodles. The following is a famous Cantonese noodle dish made from rice flour instead of the usual wheat flour. The only change I make in the recipe is that I substitute rice flour by using Swansdown cake flour (no other flour can be used) because it is readily available and the texture comes closest to that of rice flour.

Stuffed Rice Noodle Rolls (Guen Fun)

Yield: 1 doz noodle rolls

Dough: 1 recipe of rice noodle dough *(pg 10)*

Filling:

    2 cups thinly sliced cooked ham
    1 lb bean sprouts
    2 stalks green onion
    2 eggs
    ½ tsp salt

To make filling: Blanch bean sprouts in 4 cups boiling water for 15 seconds. Rinse under cold water and drain well. Shred green onions and cut into 1 inch strips. Beat eggs and salt thoroughly. Thinly coat bottom of small skillet with egg mixture (approximately 2 tbsp.). Cook over medium heat until set. Turn out on plate and continue making the egg crepes until all the beaten egg mixture is used. Cut crepes into thin strips. Divide ingredients into 12 portions.

Assembling: Referring to the basic rice noodle recipe on page 10, as each pan of the cooked *fun* is cooled, carefully remove from pan by rolling the fun jelly roll style. Unroll cooked *fun* on a plate or any flat surface, spread lower half of *fun* with one portion each of the ham, bean sprouts, green onions and egg strips. Roll up jellyroll style and cut into 1 inch sections.

Do ahead notes: *Guen Fun* is perfect for entertaining. They can be made 1 day ahead and should be served at room temperature. Drizzle a little light-soy sauce and sesame oil on top for added flavor. You may store them overnight at room temperature (on a cool day) or refrigerate.

The origins of many dim sum recipes are often found in the food traditionally served during Chinese festivities. These recipes are handed down from generation to generation within the family and many families guard them jealously. During a festival occasion, each family would share these delectable goodies with relatives and friends. One such recipe is Deep Fried Pork Turnovers (*Hom Suey Gok* or *Gai Loan*). The pastry of the turnover is made from glutinous rice flour. The dough is very chewy and soft inside, yet crispy and crunchy on the outside because it is deep fried. As a child growing up in my father's village, I helped my aunt wrap hundreds of these turnovers for a multitude of occasions such as birthdays, New Years, weddings, etc. Today, it is one of the most popular items on a tea lunch menu.

Deep Fried Pork Turnovers (Hom Suey Gok) 咸水角

Yield: 2½ doz

Dough:

1 recipe of salty glutinous rice dough (*pg. 11*)

Filling:

⅓ cup dried shrimp
¼ cup salted turnip, finely minced
1 cup fresh pork, finely minced
6-7 small dried mushrooms
10-12 water chestnuts, finely minced
1 stalk green onion, minced
1 tsp sugar
1 tsp salt
1 tsp light soy sauce

½ cup sesame seeds
4 cups oil

To make filling: Soak mushrooms and dried shrimp in separate containers for 1 hour or until soft. Discard stems of mushrooms and finely dice caps. Finely dice soaked shrimp. Stir fry together for 2 minutes: dried shrimp, salted turnip and mushrooms in 1 tbsp. oil with ½ tsp. each of salt and sugar. Set aside. Add 1 tbsp. oil and stir fry pork until done, adding 1 tsp. light soy sauce, ½ tsp. salt and ½ tsp. sugar. Set aside. Now mix all ingredients together in a bowl and cool before wrapping.

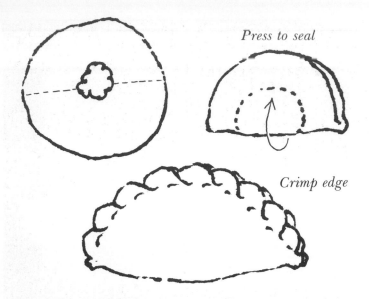

Press to seal

Crimp edge

Wrapping: Pinch off a small piece of dough, the size of a walnut and roll in your palms until it becomes a ball. Flatten slightly and roll out to a 3 inch round disc about ⅛ inch thick. (During rolling, if the dough becomes sticky, flour lightly with potato flour.) Place 1 tsp. filling in center. Bring opposite sides together and pinch to form a semi circle. For a fancier appearance, pleat or flute edge by pressing it with your thumb nail. Press sesame seeds on both sides.

Deep frying: Heat oil on medium-high heat. Deep-fry turnovers for 3-4 minutes or until they float. They will brown slightly due to the small amount of potato flour added to the dough. Drain on paper towels and serve hot.

Talk about jealously guarded recipes! I have searched through just about every Chinese cookbook available and none had the following recipe. I asked around and drew a blank wall. Even my aunt didn't know how to make it. Yet, it is served in every tea house and sold in every Chinatown bakery! But I am a very stubborn person when it comes to cooking, in that I don't give up easily. I must have tried at least a dozen or more times (the first half dozen or more

ending up in the garbage disposal!) and, finally, a breakthrough! Here it is! Now my family can enjoy (and I hope yours will too) the *Bok Tong Go* without having to drive all the way to Chinatown. (If you are lucky enough to have one close to you!)

Sweet Rice Pudding Cake (Bok Tong Go)

Yield: 2 8 inch round pudding cakes

1 cup long grain rice
1½ cup sugar
1½ cup water
1 cake compressed yeast

Preparation: Soak rice in water (have sufficient water to cover 1 inch above level of rice) for 2 days. Drain well. Mix compressed yeast with ½ cup lukewarm water. Add ¼ cup sugar. Cover and set in warm place while you do the next step.

Put ⅓ of the soaked rice and ⅓ cup water into blender and blend at high speed until rice is liquified and mixture is smooth (about 3 to 4 minutes). Set aside in mixing bowl. Blend remaining rice and water by ⅓ cup quantities, setting aside each portion into the same mixing bowl. Now pour the entire mixture back into blender and add 1¼ cups sugar. Blend at high speed for 2 more minutes. Add yeast mixture and blend at low speed for 30 seconds. Pour into mixing bowl, cover and leave in a warm place until mixture is bubbly and almost double in bulk (about 1½ to 2 hours).

Steaming: Start water in steamer boiling. Lightly stir batter again to mix evenly. Pour batter into round or square cake pan to about ½ inch high. Steam for 12-15 minutes. Cool completely. Lightly rub a little oil on top to give it a glossy appearance. Cut into diamond shape. Pudding is eaten when it is at room temperature.

Sweet Rice Pudding Cake (Bok Tong Go)

Do-ahead notes: *Bok Tong Go* is a perfect dessert recipe, since it must cool completely before serving. The pudding cake will keep for 2-3 days at room temperature.

Comments: The rice needs to be soaked for 2 days so it will be easily liquified. The fermenting process is extremely important, so don't hurry it. The textural appearance in the cross section of the pudding cake should be one full of holes (air pockets) throughout. I've tried using rice flour, but it has a much coarser texture and a most unpleasant odor. The recipe itself appears deceptively simple. The secret is in the proper proportion of ingredients and technique in combining them.

THE INNOVATORS

Even though the following dim sums are grouped as innovators, many of them are as well known as those found in the "Three Bs" section and have been standard items in tea houses for a good number of years. I have grouped them according to cooking methods in the hope that it will be easier for you to locate your favorites.

You will notice there are several northern Chinese items such as *Kuo Teh* (Pot Stickers) and Mandarin Onion Pancakes, which are usually not found in a Cantonese tea house. Nevertheless, I have included them because they are extremely good and often requested. Another northern favorite that is very close to my heart (and my stomach) is *Muu Shu* Pork. Although it is considered a dinner fare, I've often served (and really preferred) it as a main luncheon course.

To further tease your ever curious palate and really live up to the name of this chapter, I have created several "innovations" of my own, just for you. You must try my Chicken Lollipops, mouth watering and highly aromatic deep fried chicken drummettes marinated in five spice powder and fresh garlic; Mini Chicken Rolls and savory Pork Triangles, two sinfully delicious (because you can't stop eating them) deep fried dumplings with wrappings as light as angel's wings; Shrimp Boats, a spectacular and scrumptious dish that a 10 year old child can make in his sleep; and my special Chinese Beef Jerky, a favorite in my family and a nutritious snack for everyone.

Marinated Meats And Vegetables

Parchment Chicken (Gee Bow Gai)

Yield: 16 wrapping packets

紙包雞

1 whole chicken breast
1 tsp dark soy sauce
½ tsp sherry
1 tbsp minced green onion
1 tsp minced fresh ginger root
½ tsp sesame oil
5 dashes hot sauce
½ tsp salt
1 tbsp sugar
1 tsp cornstarch
¼ tsp garlic juice
1 tbsp minced Chinese parsley *(cilentro)*
4 cups oil
Cooking parchment

Preparation: Partially freeze chicken breast and slice it paper thin, across the grain, into narrow strips. Marinate chicken in the rest of the ingredients for several hours or overnight. Cut cooking parchment into 4 inch squares.

Wrapping: Position parchment with corners at top, bottom, left and right. Drop about 1 tbsp. of filling on lower corner of parchment. Tuck lower corner under filling and fold parchment about ⅓ way up. Fold left and right corners toward center, flatten filling and fold parchment paper once toward top corner. Tuck in top corner.

Cooking: Heat oil in wok. Drop wrapped chicken in oil and fry for 1½ to 2 minutes *at the most*. Drain on paper towel and serve hot.

Do-ahead notes: Deep fry, cool and freeze. To reheat, preheat oven at 350°. Heat frozen packets for 7-8 minutes.

Comments: Foil may be substituted if parchment paper is unavailable. You may also use cellophane paper, and that's quite pretty as the filling shows through clearly. The advantage of using the parchment paper is that the chicken pieces will not stick to the wrapper. If you prefer to serve fresh, wrap the filling several hours ahead and deep-fry at the last minute.

Spicy Spareribs in Black Bean Sauce (Dow See Mon Pie Quat)

豆豉排骨

Yield: 4 servings

1 lb spareribs
2 cloves garlic, finely minced
2 tbsp salted black beans
1 tbsp fresh ginger, minced
1 tsp dark soy sauce
½-¾ cup chicken broth
1 tsp cornstarch
2 tbsp sherry
1 tbsp chili oil
Chinese parsley (*cilentro*)

Preparation: Have butcher cut spareribs into ¾ inch sections. Trim off fat. Wash and rinse black beans 2 or 3 times, then mash them with garlic, ginger and soy sauce. Mix cornstarch with sherry.

Cooking: Heat chili oil in wok and brown spareribs with the black bean mixture for 2 minutes or so. Add chicken broth, cover and simmer on low heat for 35

minutes. Check every once in a while to make sure there's liquid in the wok. Add more broth if necessary. After 35 minutes of simmering, there should be about ¼ cup liquid left and spareribs are ready. Add the cornstarch mixture and stir until sauce thickens. Correct seasonings and serve in small dishes. Garnish with a sprig of Chinese parsley.

Do ahead notes: Spareribs can be made and reheated in wok or skillet.

Barbecued Pork (Cha Siu)

义燒

Yield: Good for a crowd

1 3-3½ lb boneless pork butt
2 tbsp *hoisin* sauce
4 tbsp catsup
4 tbsp sugar
1 tsp salt
1 tbsp dark soy sauce
¼ tsp salt peter

Preparation: Cut pork butt into 4 inch by 2 inch by 1 inch strips. Mix rest of ingredients and rub over pork pieces. Marinate at least 4 hours or overnight.

Cooking: Preheat oven at 375°. Line roasting pan with foil and place pork on roasting rack. Roast a total of 45 minutes, turning over once or twice.

Do-ahead notes: Barbecued pork can be made anywhere from a few days to 2 weeks in advance. Just wrap and freeze. For cold appetizers, thaw, then slice just before serving. To reheat, thaw first and reheat in a slow oven until just heated through (about 20 minutes). Delicious either way.

Comments: Barbecued pork can be used in fried rice, egg rolls, filling for steamed pork buns, stir fry with vegetables and as garnishes for many noodle dishes.

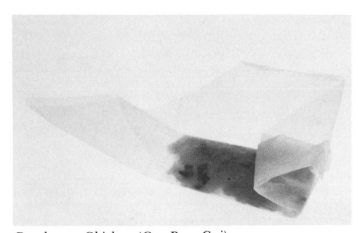

Parchment Chicken (Gee Bow Gai)

Spareribs in Black Bean Sauce (Dow See Pie Quat)

Barbecued Pork (Cha Siu)

Chicken Lollipops (Jow Nn Hueng Gui)

Beef Jerky (Gnow Yoke Gone)

Curried Chicken Wings (Ga Lei Gai Yik)

Chicken Lollipops
(Jow Nn Heung Gai)

Yield: 20 chicken drummettes

20 chicken drummettes (the upper parts of the wing)

Meat marinade:
1 tsp 5-spice powder
1½ tsp salt
1-2 cloves garlic, finely minced
1 tbsp ginger, finely minced

炸
五
香
雞

Coating mixture:
⅓ cup flour
⅓ cup cornstarch
¼ tsp white pepper
¼ tsp 5 spice powder
¼ tsp paprika

4 cups oil

Preparation: Separate the skin and tendons attached to the narrow end of the drummette and push the meat down towards the thick end. You now have a "lollipop." Repeat procedure for the rest of the drummettes. Mix with meat marinade and let stand for 4 hours or overnight. Mix coating.

Cooking: Heat oil in wok over medium high heat. Coat lollipops in flour mixture, then deep fry until golden brown. Drain on paper towels and serve hot.

Do ahead notes: Lollipops can be deep fried then frozen. To reheat, heat oven at 425°. Spread frozen lollipops on cookie sheet and reheat for 15 minutes or so. A faster method is to thaw out and deep-fry again briefly.

Comments: Do not over cook the chicken. It only takes about 3 minutes or a little more to cook through. These make great hors d'oeuvres.

Chinese Beef Jerky is a favorite snack in China. The flavor is a bit on the sweet side compared to its western counterpart and definitely not spicy. You can purchase ready made jerkies in Chinatown. However, in case there is not one near you, here's a home made recipe I enjoy sharing.

Beef Jerky (Gnow Yoke Gone)

Yield: ¼ lb jerky

½ lb flank steak
1 tsp salt
2 tsp sherry
4 tsp honey
3 tbsp sugar
1 tbsp each of: catsup, *hoisin* sauce, oyster sauce, light soy sauce, dark soy sauce
2 pinches of salt peter

牛
肉
乾

Preparation: Partially freeze meat first, then thinly slice beef. Marinate in rest of ingredients for at least 1 day.

Cooking: Bake single layer at 250° for 45-55 minutes.

Do ahead notes: Make ahead and serve later.

Comments: These never last for more than 1 hour in my family. As hard as I've tried, I've never had any for more than 2 days. (I have to hide them from my children, especially the big one—my husband!)

Curried Chicken Wings
(Ga Lei Gai Yik)

Yield: 4 dinner servings

10 chicken wings
2 medium Russet potatoes
1 medium yellow onion
1 clove garlic, crushed
1 chunk crushed ginger (size of a quarter)
2 tbsp oil
1 tsp salt
1 tbsp curry
1 tbsp sugar
2 tbsp sherry
½ cup chicken broth
2 tbsp oyster sauce
1 tbsp catsup
2 stalks green onions, cut into 1 inch lengths

Preparation: Cut off chicken wing tips and save for stock. Cut wings at joint. Peel and cut potatoes into chunks and slice onion into small wedges.

Cooking: In a heavy bottomed 3 quart sauce pot, heat 2 tbsp. oil and brown ginger, garlic and chicken wings for 4 minutes. Add rest of ingredients except green onions. Bring to a boil and simmer for ½ hour on low heat. Add the green onions the last 5 minutes.

Do ahead notes: Cook early in the day. Chicken and potatoes taste better after several hours in the sauce. It's great the next day.

Comments: Some people are quite surprised that we use potatoes in our cooking. It is quite a common vegetable in southern China, although we don't serve it the same way as the westerners do. Curry is the most popular seasoning for potatoes. Another is 5 spice powder. (*See page 81.*)

Pickled Mustard Greens
(Suen Gai Choy)

Yield: 2 1 qt jars

2 qts mustard greens cut into 1 inch pieces
4 slices ginger root

Pickling mixtures:
3 cups water
1 cup sugar
4 tsp salt
⅔ cup cider vinegar

Preparation: Bring pickling mixture to a boil. Simmer for a few minutes until sugar and salt are dissolved. Set aside to cool completely.

Break side branches off the center stalk of the mustard greens. Tear off leaves and save them for soup. Using only the branches, cut 1 inch to 1½ inch chunks. Blanch them in a pot of boiling water for 1 minute. Rinse under cold water. Drain and let cool completely.

In two 1 quart glass jars (cleaned and rinsed with hot water) place mustard greens and 2 slices of fresh ginger root and fill with the cooled pickling mixture. Cover and refrigerate for one week. Serve chilled as a side dish.

Do ahead notes: These keep well in refrigerator for several months, except they will be munched up long before then.

Comments: The last time I served the pickled mustard greens for a tea lunch, the 8 of us ate up 2 full jars! Have plenty on hand!

Deep Fried Dumplings

A taste of any of the following deep fried goodies and you'll be on the road of no return! Don't say I didn't warn you.

Crispy Taro Turnovers (Wu Gok)

Yield: 24-26 turnovers

Taro pastry:
    4 cups cooked and mashed *taro* (about 2 lbs
        raw)
    2 tsp salt
    1 tsp sugar
    ¼ tsp white pepper
    ¼ tsp 5-spice powder
    7-8 tbsp potato flour

To make pastry: Peel, then slice *taro* into thin slices. Steam taro for 30-40 minutes until soft. Finely mash and add seasonings. Mix in potato flour last. The mixture should be just stiff enough to handle, but be careful not to over work it or it will be too mushy.

Filling:
    ½ lb finely minced pork

Meat marinade:
    ½ tsp 5-spice powder
    1 tsp sherry
    1 tsp dark soy sauce
    1 tsp cornstarch
    ½ tsp sesame oil

    ½ cup bamboo shoots, finely minced
    1 stalk green onion, chopped
    2 tsp oil
    ¾ tsp salt
    1¼ tsp sugar
    ⅛ tsp white pepper

Sauce mixture:
    1 tsp cornstarch
    2 tsp chicken broth or water
    2 tsp sherry

    1 cup all purpose flour

To make filling: Marinate minced pork with meat marinade for 15 minutes. Mix sauce. Stir fry pork with bamboo shoots and green onions in 2 tsp. oil. Add all other seasonings then pour in the sauce mixture. Stir until it thickens. Mix well and chill for 2 hours in refrigerator.

Wrapping: Take about 2 tbsp. of the taro mixture, roll into a ball and flatten out to a 3 inch circle. Place 1 tbsp. filling in center and bring the opposite sides to seal. Continue making the turnovers until all of the pastry and filling is used up. Place turnovers on platter with seam side up.

Deep frying: Heat 4 cups oil in wok over medium high heat. Dredge turnovers in flour (all purpose) and deep fry in hot oil until golden on both sides. Serve hot.

Do ahead notes: Cooked turnovers can be frozen. To reheat, thaw out to room temperature then deep fry again until crispy and golden brown. YUM!

Comments: Taro is the tuberous root of a tropical plant bearing flowers on a fleshy spike surrounded by a hoodlike leaf. The texture of taro is similar to a potato in that they are both starchy. However, taro is much smoother, lighter and far more delicate. Taro is available year round in Chinatown stores, at least on the West Coast; they are shipped from Hawaii. This is the same root with which the islanders make *poi*, the counterpart of rice to the Chinese.

Shrimp Toast (Ha Toe See)

Yield: 2 doz

½ lb fresh prawns
6 slices white sandwich bread
2 pieces 1 inch square fresh pork fat
8 water chestnuts
3 tbsp cornstarch
1 tsp salt
2 tbsp sherry
1 small egg, lightly beaten
2 stalks green onions, finely chopped
Sesame seeds
Paprika

Preparation: Leave bread out on a platter for 2 hours to dry. Trim crusts and cut each slice into 4 squares. Shell, de vein and clean prawns. Mince them into a fine, pulp like paste. Chop pork fat and water chestnuts until fine. Then mix with prawns, green onions, salt, sherry, cornstarch and beaten egg. Mix well and spread mixture on the bread, making a slight mound on each piece. Sprinkle sesame seeds and paprika on the filling and press lightly so they adhere to the mixture.

Cooking: Heat 4 cups of oil in the wok. Drop bread, shrimp side down, into oil and fry for 30 seconds. Turn and fry on the other side for another 30 seconds. (This is estimated time, since it depends on how hot the oil is. Use your judgment.) Both sides should be golden. Drain on paper towel and serve hot.

Do ahead notes: Deep fry bread and mixture until it becomes a light beige color, then cool and freeze. To reheat, preheat oven at 350°, place frozen toast in a single layer on a cookie sheet and heat for 12 minutes. If toast already is thawed, reheat for 5 to 6 minutes. The toast will become a deeper brown as it's reheated.

Comments: Another way to serve this toast is by cutting each piece of bread diagonally into 2 triangles and spread on mixture. Top with a halved prawn in a lemon twist fashion and deep fry as usual. Arrange toast on a round platter, pin wheel fashion. Top with cherry tomatoes or parsley sprigs in the center of the pinwheel.

Shrimp Turnovers (Jow Ha Gok)

Yield: 2 to 2½ doz

Dough:
1 recipe of glutinous rice dough (*pg. 11*)

Filling:
¾ lb shrimp, shelled, de veined & minced
2 tbsp pork fat
10 water chestnuts
¼ cup salted turnips, finely minced
1 stalk green onion, finely minced
¼ cup Chinese parsley (*cilentro*), finely chopped
¾ tsp salt
½ tsp sugar
¼ tsp white pepper
1 tbsp cornstarch
2 tbsp sherry

To make filling: Mince pork fat with water chestnuts then add shrimp and mince together. Mix with rest of ingredients.

Wrapping: Pinch off a small piece of dough, the size of a walnut, and roll in your palms until it becomes a ball. Flatten slightly and roll out to a 3 inch round disc about ⅛ inch thick. (During rolling, if the dough becomes sticky, flour lightly with potato flour.) Place 1 teaspoonful filling in center. Bring opposite sides together and pinch to form a semi circle. For a fancier appearance, pleat or flute edge by pressing it with your thumb nail. Press sesame seeds on both sides.

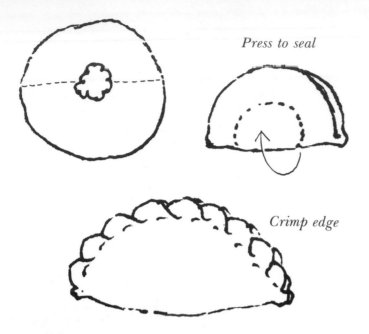

Press to seal

Crimp edge

Deep frying: Heat oil on medium high heat. Deep fry for 3 to 4 minutes or until turnovers float. They will brown slightly due to the small amount of potato flour added to the dough. Drain on paper towels and serve hot.

In the beginning, cooking methods and ideas were pretty much confined and usually limited to the availability of food stuffs and accumulated knowledge of local inhabitants. As time progressed, people began to travel and explore. Trading flourished. We've already seen how ravioli owes its beginning to Marco Polo's historic China trip. This is just one example of how travel and trading has influenced food and cooking throughout the world, so that, today, the ethnic cuisine of one country may bear striking similarity to that of another country whose people and culture are totally different.

Since so much trading and borrowing of ideas has been going on, I may as well get in on the act. I have always been fascinated by the *filo* dough (or leaves) found in the famous Greek pastry, *baklava*.

This extremely thin and delicate pastry dough fascinates me so much that I finally had to find out how difficult it would be to work with. Much to my surprise, it is not half as difficult as I expected. I am delighted to share with you the following two original recipes I concocted one Sunday afternoon sometime ago.

Working With Filo

Filo dough (or leaves), is a tissue thin Greek pastry dough made of egg, flour and water. Filo can be found in almost all delicatessens or gourmet shops. They are usually frozen when purchased. Just leave them in the refrigerator for 24 hours or more until the leaves thaw out. Take out only the amount called for in the recipe and keep the rest well wrapped.

To prevent filo leaves from drying out while you work, lay out a slightly damp cloth on the counter, then a sheet of plastic wrap over it. Place the leaves on top. Cover them first with a plastic wrap, then with another slightly damp cloth. It is not a good idea to lay the leaves directly on a damp cloth because the moisture will turn the dough soggy. That's why the plastic wrap is placed in between.

Make sure you have the filling and all other ingredients ready. I find my pastry brush is a little too rough for brushing the oil on the dough. Instead, I smooth oil on with my fingers. It goes much faster and there is no problem of breakage. Even if you break a filo leaf, just glue it together with oil and it stays put by the time you roll it up. Of course, if you were doing western recipes, melted butter is the usual moistening agent between each leaf.

Keep the wrapped triangles or rolls moist by covering them with a plastic wrap. You can either bake them or deep fry them. I prefer the latter method as they are much quicker to do and the texture is crisper and lighter.

Pickled Mustard Greens (Suen Gai Choy)

Shrimp Toast (Ha Toe See)

Shrimp Turnovers (Jow Ha Gok)

Mini Chicken Rolls (Gai Guen)

Savory Pork Triangles (Gee Yoke Gok)

Seafood Stuffed Bell Peppers (Ha Yu Jeung Lot Jiu)

Mini Chicken Rolls (Gai Guen)

Yield: 1½ doz

鶏巻

1 chicken breast, finely minced
8 water chestnuts, finely minced
1-4 oz can of mushrooms, finely minced
2 stalks green onions, finely minced
1 tbsp cornstarch
1 tsp light soy sauce
1 tsp sesame oil
½ tsp white vinegar
½ tsp sugar
½ tsp salt
½ tsp sherry
1 tsp oyster sauce
1 tbsp fresh ginger, finely minced
9 sheets of *filo* dough
4 cups oil
1 beaten egg

Preparation: Mix all ingredients except the last 3. Let flavor intermingle for several hours or overnight.

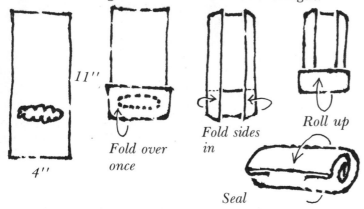

11''
4''

Fold over once

Fold sides in

Roll up

Seal

Wrapping: Cut filo dough lengthwise into 4 equal strips (each about 4 inches to 4½ inches wide). Brush 1 strip with a little oil (I use my fingers) and lay another strip on top. Brush the second strip with same amount of oil. Place 1 tbsp filling on 1 end of the strip, shaping filling into a cylinder. Roll filling up once, then fold left and right side of strip ½ inch lengthwise to enclose the filling. Continue rolling filling all the way to the end of strip. Seal with beaten egg. Repeat procedure with rest of the filo dough.

Cooking: Heat oil in wok over medium high heat. Deep fry chicken rolls until golden. Drain on paper towels. Cool slightly before serving.

Do ahead notes: Cook ahead. Keeps crisp for 2 hours. Good at room temperature also. To reheat, briefly deep fry in wok again or in preheated 350° oven for 7 to 8 minutes. Rolls can also be refrigerated. But be sure to bring them back to room temperature before deep frying again, unless you are reheating by oven, in which case, they can go directly from refrigerator to oven.

Comments: These are so good you will not be able to stop eating them until they are ALL GONE! Following is a variation in which I use fresh pork.

Same ingredients as in the chicken recipe, only I substitute ½ lb. pork (finely minced). Marinate pork in the same seasoning as in the chicken recipe. Stir fry pork in 1 tsp. oil and stir in the following sauce mixture: 1 tbsp. each of cornstarch and chicken broth; ¼ tsp. vinegar; ½ tsp. each of light soy sauce, sherry and sesame oil. Cool mixture completely before wrapping.

Savory Pork Triangles (Gee Yoke Gok)

Yield: 3 doz

½ lb fresh ground pork
12 water chestnuts, finely minced
2 stalks green onions, finely minced
½ tsp salt
½ tsp sugar
½ tsp sesame oil
1 tsp catsup
1 tsp dark soy sauce

1 tsp sherry
2 tsp *hoisin* sauce
9 sheets (leaves) *filo* dough
1 beaten egg
4 cups oil

Preparation: Brown pork with minced water chestnuts until done, drain off fat, return to heat and add green onions and all seasonings. Stir until flavor is well blended. Cool in refrigerator several hours or over night until completely chilled before wrapping.

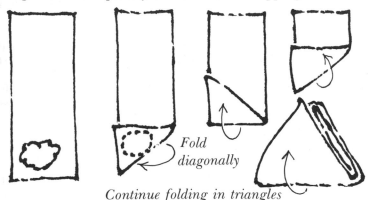

Fold diagonally

Continue folding in triangles

Wrapping: Cut filo into 4 even strips lengthwise. (They should be about 4 inches to 4½ inches wide). Fold each strip in half lengthwise and lubricate the dough with a little oil. (Use your fingers) Place 1 tsp. filling on the bottom corner of the strip. Fold up corner to form a triangle. Continue folding in triangles until the entire length of dough is folded. Seal end with beaten egg. Repeat procedure with rest of the filo dough.

Cooking: Heat oil in wok over medium high heat. Deep fry triangles until just golden. Drain on paper towel. Cool slightly before serving.

Do-ahead notes: Same as the previous recipe.

Comments: These are so good that, the first time I made them, all 36 were devoured, not by myself alone, thank God, but by my family in less then 10 minutes!

Pan Fried Morsels

Eat, drink and be merry, for tomorrow you'll throw away your scale!

Medallion Mushrooms (Gum Chin Doan Goo)

Yield: 24-30

24-30 medium sized fresh mushrooms
1 cup lean ground pork
4 medium sized prawns
6-8 water chestnuts, finely chopped
1 tbsp dark soy sauce
1 tbsp sherry
½ tsp salt
½ tsp sugar
1 tsp cornstarch
2 tsp oil
½ cup chicken stock
4-5 tbsp oyster sauce
1 stalk green onion, chopped

金錢蔘如

Preparation: Wash and stem mushrooms. (Save stems for something else.) Pat dry. Shell and de vein prawns. Mince them and mix with water chestnuts, pork, soy sauce, sherry, sugar, salt and cornstarch. Spread about 1 tsp. of filling onto each mushroom.

Cooking: Heat 2 tsp. oil in a skillet and place mushrooms in a single layer with the filling facing up. Brown for 1 minute. Pour ½ cup stock into the skillet, cover and simmer for 8-10 minutes, adding more stock if necessary. Uncover. (There should be about ¼ cup stock left in the skillet.) Add oyster sauce and baste the mushrooms. When sauce thickens, transfer to platter and garnish with chopped green onions.

Do ahead notes: This dish can be made ahead of time and reheated *slowly* on the stove, adding a little more broth and oyster sauce to make certain the sauce is not dried out.

Comments: Pick mushrooms that are about 1½ to 2 inches in diameter since they shrink during cooking. Insert toothpicks when serving as appetizers. *Gum Chin Doan Goo* can double as a dinner side dish.

Seafood Stuffed Bell Peppers (Ha Yu Yeung Lot Jiu)

Yield: 2 doz

Seafood mixture:
   ¼ lb fish filet (rock cod, butter fish, red
       snapper, etc.)
   8 medium sized prawns, shelled &
       de veined
   1 stalk green onion, finely minced
   ½ tsp salt
   2 dashes white pepper
   1 small egg white
   1 tsp cornstarch

3 small green peppers
Paprika powder

Sauce mixture:
   1 tsp cornstarch
   ½ cup chicken broth
   1 tsp light soy sauce
   ½ tsp sesame oil
   ½ tsp sugar

½ cup chicken broth
1-2 tbsp oil

Preparation: Mince prawns with fish and green onion until texture is a fine paste. Add remainder of seafood mixture and mix well. Wash and cut bell peppers in halves lengthwise. Seed them but do not wash the inside (stuffing will adhere better). Cut each half into quarters. Fill with seafood mixture. Lightly sprinkle with paprika powder. Cook sauce mixture in a separate sauce pan.

Cooking: In a 10 inch or 12 inch skillet, heat 1 or 2 tbsp. oil at medium high heat. Brown stuffed pepper, filling side down, for 1 minute or a little longer until slightly brown. Add ½ cup chicken stock and turn stuffed pepper filling side up. Continue cooking at medium high heat for 2-3 minutes. (If broth evaporates too fast, add a little more. There should be very little broth left.) Add the cooked sauce mixture. Heat for another minute or so until sauce is bubbly. Transfer stuffed peppers to serving platter and pour sauce over them. Serve hot.

Do ahead notes: Do through preparation

Comments: The stuffing can be made entirely of fish. I find the prawns give it extra flavor. If you would like to spice up the sauce, add ½ to 1 tsp. chili oil and ½ tsp. vinegar to the mixture. Wow!

The Cook's Mistake

Pot Stickers have long been a favorite northern Chinese luncheon snack. There is a charming story attributed to their origin which I will share with you.

There once was a chef who worked in the royal household. The chef was a very old man and he was training his son to take his place. One day, the old man was making some dumplings for the royal family and, being a little senile, he forgot about the dumplings until he heard the wok sizzling alarmingly on the stove. When he uncovered the wok, all the dumplings were browned on the bottom! The old man was panic stricken. How can one serve burnt food to the Emperor!? His head would be chopped off for sure! But his son saw the predicament and, to save his father from possible harm, he himself presented the dish to the Emperor. The Emperor wanted to know why his food was burnt. The son, who was a very quick witted fellow, explained that this was his new recipe called Pot Stickers, and that the bottom of each dumpling is supposed to be nice and brown. The Emperor liked the crunchiness of the crusty bottom, and are we glad of that old man's mistake!

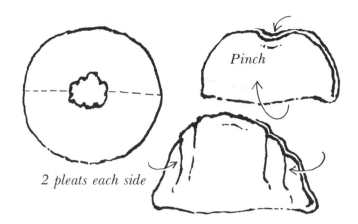

2 pleats each side

Pot Stickers (Kuo Teh)

鍋
貼

Yield: 4 doz

Dough:
4 cups sifted all purpose flour
1 cup & 2 tbsp warm water

To make dough: Mix flour with warm water and knead for 10 to 15 minutes. There is no need to add any flour on the board as you knead because the dough should be at a perfect consistency. Let dough rest for 20 minutes while you make the filling.

Filling:
1 lb fresh ground pork
1 pkg (10 oz) frozen chopped spinach
1 tbsp light soy sauce
1 tbsp sherry
1 tbsp sesame oil
1¼ tsp salt
3 tbsp minced green onions
3 tbsp minced fresh ginger
3 tbsp minced Chinese parsley (*cilentro*)

To make filling: Partially thaw spinach and lightly squeeze out liquid (leave some liquid with the spinach). Mix with rest of ingredients.

Wrapping: Divide dough into 4 parts. Roll each part out to about 12 inches in length and divide into 12 balls. Roll each ball into 3 inch round flat discs and drop 1 tbsp. of filling in center. Fold the dough over the filling, pinching together just the top to make a half circle. On the side nearest you, form 2 to 3 pleats on each side and pinch them to meet the opposite side to seal.

Cooking: Heat 2 tbsp. of oil in a 12 inch heavy skillet over medium high heat. Lightly brown Pot Stickers until golden on the bottom, pour 1 cup water into the skillet and cover immediately. Cook over medium heat until most of the liquid is absorbed. Uncover and continue cooking until liquid is completely absorbed and the Pot Stickers are golden brown on the bottom. Serve with the following dip: 2 tbsp. light soy sauce, 1 tsp. sesame oil and 1 tbsp. vinegar. Another good dip is chili oil.

Do ahead notes: Wrap and freeze them. Cook just before serving. Pot Stickers turn out even better when the freezing process gives the filling additional moisture, making them juicier and tastier! Add 5-7 more minutes to cooking time if frozen.

Comments: To prevent Pot Stickers from actually sticking to the bottom of the pan, it is best to use either a Teflon, a heavy bottom commercial aluminum, a cast iron or a well seasoned steel skillet.

Onion Pancakes (Choan Yao Bang)

Yield: 6 4 inch pancakes

葱
油
餅

⅔ cup flour
¼ cup lukewarm water
2 stalks green onions, chopped
3 tbsp dehydrated onion
3 strips cooked & crumbled bacon
lard
salt
sesame seeds
2-3 tbsp oil

Preparation: Soak dry onion for 20 minutes. Discard water. Mix with chopped green onions and crumbled bacon.

To make pancakes: Mix flour with water and knead for 5 minutes. Separate into 6 parts and roll each into a 4 inch round flat dough. Spread a thin layer of lard on the dough and sprinkle salt and 1 tbsp. filling. Roll up jelly roll style, pull lightly on both ends to stretch slightly lengthwise. Now coil it around in a snake like fashion and tuck ends under. Roll out again to 4 inch rounds. Spread some sesame seeds on the bottom as you roll, so they adhere to the pancake.

Cooking: Heat skillet on medium heat, add 1 tsp. oil. Brown slowly on both sides until golden. Repeat with rest of the pancakes, adding a little oil as needed. Serve while hot.

Do ahead notes: Cook ahead and refrigerate or freeze. If frozen, thaw out first. Then reheat single layer for 5 minutes in preheated 400° oven or in skillet until thoroughly heated. Great hors d'oeuvres!

Comments: Do not brown bacon until crisp. Cook until firm only. (If too crisp, the flavor is cooked out.) Finely mince bacon. Pancakes are good either as luncheon side dishes (serving them whole) or as hors d'oeuvres (cutting each pancake into quarters). The traditional version does not include bacon, but I happen to like the bacon taste.

Mini Stuffed Potato Cakes (See Jai Bang)

薯
仔
餅

Yield: 24 mini cakes

Potato pastry:
2 cups cooked & mashed potatoes (about 1-1¼ lb)
1 tsp salt
½ tsp sugar
⅛ tsp white pepper
¼ tsp 5-spice powder

To make pastry: Steam sliced potatoes for ½ hour or until soft. Transfer to mixing bowl, mash and mix with rest of the seasonings.

Filling:
½ cup minced barbecued pork or ham
⅓ cup minced water chestnuts
3 tbsp minced green onions
2 tsp oil
¼ tsp salt
1 tsp sugar
⅛ tsp white pepper
¼ tsp 5 spice powder
½ tsp sherry
½ tsp light soy sauce

Chinese parsley (*cilentro*)

To make filling: Heat 2 tsp. oil in wok or skillet, stir fry pork, water chestnuts and green onions for 1 minute and add rest of ingredients. Mix well and cool for at least 2 hours in the refrigerator.

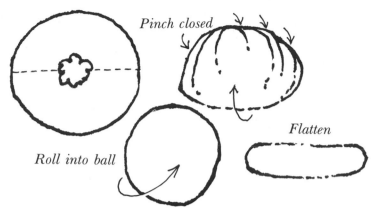

Pinch closed

Flatten

Roll into ball

Wrapping: Scoop about 1 tbsp. potato pastry, roll into a ball and flatten in your palms to a 2 inch round. Put a tsp. of filling in the middle, bring opposite sides together, pinch to seal and lightly flatten to size of a half dollar. Press a Chinese parsley leaf on both sides for decoration. Repeat procedure for rest of filling.

Cooking: Over medium high heat, brown Mini Potato Cakes on each side with a little oil. Serve with a mixture of light soy sauce, sesame oil and vinegar, or Chinese mustard dip.

Do-ahead notes: Cook ahead and reheat in skillet with a little oil. Brown on both sides.

Comments: This is an offspring of the Crispy Taro Turnovers on page 30. Since *taro* is not readily available in many parts of the United States and is also a seasonal vegetable, I sometimes make this recipe for my family. However, mashed potatoes do not hold together when deep fried, and that's why I make these pan fried cakes. You must try this recipe as soon as you can. Your family will love it and what a way to dress up the lowly potato!

Muu Shu Pork resembles the Mexican burrito in that both are fillings wrapped in a tortilla like wrapper. The Chinese filling is made of pork and stir fried vegetables and the Muu Shu Pork wrapper is much thinner than the tortilla.

Muu Shu Pork

Yield: Fills 12-14 small doilies (4 inch to 4½ inch)

½ lb pork, cut thin match stick size

Meat marinade:
    1 tsp cornstarch
    2 tsp dark soy sauce
    1 tsp sherry

4 dried mushrooms
2 doz lilly buds
¼ cup cloud ears
1 cup bean sprouts
1 cup bamboo shoots, cut match stick size
2 cups *napa* cabbage, shredded
2 stalks green onions, cut into ½ inch strips

Sauce mixture:
    1 tbsp cornstarch
    1 tbsp sherry
    2 tbsp oyster sauce
    1 tsp light soy sauce
    1 tsp sesame oil
    ¼ cup chicken broth

2 tbsp oil
¼ cup *hoisin* sauce
onion brushes

Preparation: Mix pork with meat marinade for ½ hour. Soak mushrooms, lilly buds and cloud ears until soft. Discard stems from mushrooms and slice caps into thin strips. Tie a knot in the middle of the lilly buds and nip off the tough ends. Pinch off the tough parts of the cloud ears and break into small pieces. Mix sauce. Make onion brushes by cutting the white part of the green onions into 3 inch lengths. Make several ½ inch cuts lengthwise on both ends. Soak in ice water for a few hours. The cut ends will flare out, resembling a brush.

Cooking: Stir fry bean sprouts for 1 minute in 1 tsp. of oil. Set aside. Add 2 tsp. oil and stir fry bamboo shoots with cabbage for 2-2½ minutes. Set aside. Add 1 tbsp. oil and stir fry pork with mushrooms, lilly buds and cloud ears until pork is done, about 2-3 minutes. Add sauce mixture, stir until thick. Add back vegetables including the green onions. Serve with Peking Doilies. (*The next recipe.*)

To serve: Spread a little hoisin sauce with the tip of the onion brush and spoon mixture on it. Wrap and eat finger style.

Do ahead notes: Muu Shu Pork mixtures can be made ahead and kept warm for ½ hour.

Comments: This is a very popular northern dish which makes excellent luncheon fare. Everything is made ahead of time so there is no last minute work. The following recipe will show you how to make the accompanying doilies.

Peking Doilies (Bork Bang)

Yield: 12-14 doilies

    1 cup sifted all purpose flour
    ¼ cup & 2 tsp boiling water
    sesame oil (or vegetable oil)

Preparation: Mix boiling water with flour and knead for 10 minutes. Let dough rest for 10 minutes. Break into 12-14 pieces. Roll each into a round ball, then flatten each with heel of the hand and brush half of the rounds with sesame or vegetable oil. Top with other half of the rounds. Roll each round to a 4 inch to 5 inch diameter.

Cooking: Heat a Teflon or a heavy bottomed skillet over medium heat. Cook doilies for 1 minute or less on each side. Doilies should turn just very lightly beige. Cool for several seconds and separate doilies as soon as you can, while they are still hot.

Do ahead notes: These can be made in advance and frozen. Steam frozen doilies for 12 minutes or, if thawed out, 6-7 minutes will do.

Comments: To make good doilies, observe the following 3 points: 1) The dough should be a bit on the "dry" side. (Not too dry or the doilies will crack, but definitely not so soft they become too mushy for rolling and separating. 2) Oil the flattened dough *well*, especially on the edges, in order to have an easier time when pulling them apart. 3) Roll doilies out and away in 1 stroke from center in all directions to insure evenness and a good round shape. Do not roll in back and forth motion, since the edges may fold in and you will have a hard time separating the doilies. After practicing on a few, you'll know what I mean.

    This is a fun project to do on a rainy day with your children. I have my children, ages 10 and 13, trained so that they are now my official doily makers!

    It would also be helpful if you have a tortilla press. Before you begin rolling the 2 doilies together (they are a bit slippery because of the oil in between), press them on the tortilla press and it will help you get started much quicker.

From Your Steamers

    Most homes in China do not have ovens for baking. Consequently, many of our snack items are either steamed or deep fried. Here are some more steamed dim sum dishes.

Steamed Rice Noodle Rolls (Gee Cheung Fun)

Taro Pudding Cake (Wu Tao Go)

Yield: 1 9 inch round cake

2 cups *taro* cut into ¼ inch cubes
1¾ cup chicken broth
1 cup Swansdown cake flour (no substitute)
½ cup pork butt, finely minced
⅓ cup Chinese sausage or cooked ham, minced
¼ cup dried shrimp, soaked & minced
2 tbsp salted turnips, minced
⅓ cup chopped green onions
⅓ cup Chinese parsley (*cilentro*), chopped
½ tsp 5 spice powder
¼ tsp white pepper
4 tsp oil
1 tsp salt

Preparation: Soak dried shrimp for ½ hour before mincing. Reserve 1 tbsp. each of the chopped green onions and Chinese parsley for topping. Heat 2 tsp. oil and stir fry pork, sausage, shrimp and salted turnips with the remaining green onions and parsley. Add 5 spice powder, white pepper and ½ tsp. salt. Set aside.

To make batter, stir fry taro cubes in 2 tsp. oil. Add ½ tsp. salt and ½ cup chicken broth. Cover and simmer for 10-15 minutes or until taro is soft. Meanwhile, mix cake flour with 1¼ cup chicken broth. When taro is done, add to batter, including whatever amount of liquid is left in the taro. Finally add the meat mixture. Stir to mix well.

Cooking: Pour batter into a 9 inch cake pan. Set in steamer and bring water to a boil. Cover. Turn heat down to simmer and steam for ½ hour. Insert toothpick in center. If it comes out clean, it is done. Garnish with reserved onions and parsley. Cool to lukewarm or room temperature before serving.

Do ahead notes: *Wu Tao Go* can be cooked ahead and refrigerated for several days or frozen. Since the pudding cake is eaten at room temperature, merely thaw cake out and warm to room temperature.

Comments: You can cut into wedges or diamond shapes for a delicious luncheon dish. For hors d'oeuvres, cut in small squares and be prepared for rave reviews! It will be one of the most unusual and delicious snacks you'll ever serve. This makes ideal picnic food too.

Steamed Rice Noodle Rolls (Gee Cheung Fun)

Yield: 12 7 inch long rolls

1 basic rice noodle dough (*fun*) on page 10.
¾ cup finely minced cooked ham
½ cup finely diced green onion
½ cup finely minced Chinese parsley (*cilentro*)
2 tbsp sesame seeds

Cooking: Follow the basic *fun* dough recipe and after ladling the ⅓ cup of batter into cake pan, sprinkle a little minced ham, green onion and Chinese parsley evenly on top. Steam for 3-4 minutes. Remove from steamer and roll up jelly roll style. Sprinkle a little sesame seeds on top. Cool, cut into 1 inch lengths and serve. Use light soy sauce and sesame oil for dips.

Do ahead notes: Another great one to do ahead for the picnic basket or cocktail hour.

Shrimp Boats (Ha Yeung Dow Fu)

Yield: 24 boats

¼ lb prawns
6 small water chestnuts
1 tbsp pork fat
½ small egg, beaten
½ tsp salt
1 tbsp sherry
1 stalk green onion, finely minced
1 box bean curd (*tofu*)

Pot Stickers (Kuo Teh)

Taro Pudding Cake (Wu Tao Go)

Sweet Bean Paste Buns (Dow Sah Bow)

Shrimp Boats (Ha Yeung Dow Fu)

Muu Shu Pork

Chinese Pork Sausage Buns (Lop Cheung Bow)

Sauce mixture:

> 1½ tsp cornstarch
> 1 tsp sherry
> 2 tsp light soy sauce
> ½ cup chicken broth
> ½ tsp sesame oil

Preparation: Shell, de vein and clean prawns. Finely mince. Mince fresh pork fat with water chestnuts until fine. Add shrimp and mince together for 1 minute. Add remainder of ingredients except tofu. Mix sauce. Drain all liquid from tofu and let stand covered in bowl at least 4 hours or over night. Cut tofu into 24 1 inch × ½ inch × ½ inch cubes. Spread about 1 tsp. mixture on each tofu. Arrange attractively on a 10 inch heat proof platter.

Cooking: Put plate on steamer rack. Cover. Bring water to a boil and turn down to simmer. Steam for 10 minutes. Meanwhile, bring sauce mixture to a boil, stirring constantly until sauce thickens. Keep warm. When shrimp is done, spoon sauce over shrimp boat, garnish with additional chopped green onions and serve.

Comments: The appearance of this dish is quite elegant and dramatic. This is equally good as a dinner side dish.

Sweet Bean Paste Bun (Dow Sah Bow)

豆沙包

Yield: 2 doz

> 1 can of sweet bean paste filling

Dough:
> ½ recipe of the basic steamed bun dough
> *(pg. 9)*

Follow directions for the steamed barbecued-pork buns on page 18. Just substitute sweet bean paste for the filling.

Chinese Pork Sausage Buns (Lop Cheung Bow)

臘腸包

Yield: 2 doz

Dough:
> ½ recipe of the basic steamed bun dough
> *(pg. 9)*

Filling:
> 6 pairs of Chinese pork sausage, cut into halves. You should have 24 3 inch sausages.

Wrapping: Divide dough into 24 balls. Roll each ball into 2 inch rounds. Place sausage in middle and fold dough over, leaving ends open. Place seam side down on square piece of wax paper. Let rise in warm place for 1 hour or so.

Cooking: Steam for 10 minutes. Pork Sausage Bun can also be baked at 350° for 20-25 minutes. Mix beaten egg whites with a little water and sugar and brush buns (to keep crust soft). Brush with melted butter when done.

Do ahead notes: Make ahead and freeze. Reheat by steaming or baking 325° in loosely wrapped foil for 25 minutes.

Comments: Chinese sausage imparts a sweet flavor rather than the spicy flavor of most other sausages. They are available in Chinatown stores. If you like liver, try liver sausages as well.

Baked Buns And Turnovers

Curry Beef Buns (Ga Lei Bow)

Yield: 2 doz

Dough:
1 recipe of steamed-bun dough (*pg. 9*)

Filling:
¾ lb lean ground beef
1 cup coarsely diced bamboo shoots
2 stalks green onions
1-2 tbsp curry powder
1 tsp salt
1 tbsp oyster sauce
2 tbsp catsup
1 tbsp oil

咖哩包

To make filling: Brown ground beef in 1 tbsp. oil with bamboo shoots until done. Add all seasonings, then green onions. Mix well and chill completely before wrapping.

Wrapping: Follow direction for steamed barbecued pork buns on page 18.

Baking: Preheat oven at 350°. Brush buns with a mixture of beaten egg white, 1 tsp. water and ¼ tsp. sugar. Bake 20-25 minutes or until buns are golden brown. Remove from oven. Brush top with butter.

Do ahead notes: Bake ahead and freeze. To reheat, thaw out at room temperature. Wrap in foil and place in warm oven for 1 hour, or slightly higher temperature for a shorter time.

Comments: This and other buns are great for picnic or lunch baskets. It turns brown bagging into a gourmet's delight.

5 Spice Chicken Buns (Nn Heung Gai Bow)

Yield: 2 doz

Dough:
1 recipe of steamed bun dough (*pg. 9*)

Filling:
1½ to 2 cups diced chicken breast

Meat marinade:
2 tsp cornstarch
½ tsp light soy sauce
½ tsp dark soy sauce
½ tsp sherry
½ tsp 5 spice powder
½ tsp bean sauce

¼ cup almond slivers
¼ cup chopped celery
¼ cup chopped onion
½ cup bamboo shoots
2 stalks green onions, chopped

Sauce mixture:
⅔ cup chicken broth
1 tbsp cornstarch
1 tbsp oyster sauce
1 tsp sesame oil
1 tsp sugar
½ tsp salt

1 tbsp oil

五香鷄包

To make filling: Mix chicken with meat marinade for ½ hour or longer. Stir fry in 1 tbsp. oil until almost done. Add vegetables and continue to stir until chicken is done. Add sauce mixture, stir until thickened, mix well and chill.

Wrapping: Follow direction for steamed barbecued pork buns on page 18.

Wow Bow!

Baking: same as curry beef buns on page 45.

Do ahead notes: same as above.

Plum Sauce Chicken Buns (Mui Jeung Gai Bow)

Yield: 2 doz

Dough:
>1 recipe of the steamed barbecue pork buns (*pg. 18*)

Filling:
>1½ to 2 cups diced chicken breast

Meat marinade:
>2 tsp cornstarch
>½ tsp light soy sauce
>½ tsp dark soy sauce
>½ tsp sherry
>1 tbsp oil

>½ cup pineapple tibbits
>¼ cup diced, cooked carrot
>¼ cup diced green pepper
>¼ cup diced sweet mixed ginger

Sauce mixture:
>3 tbsp plum sauce
>1 tbsp pineapple juice
>1 tbsp cornstarch
>1 tsp catsup
>1 tsp sugar
>1 tsp vinegar
>1 tsp salt

>1 tbsp oil

To make filling: Mix meat with marinade for ½ hour or more. Stir fry in 1 tbsp of oil until almost done. Add vegetables and stir fry for 1 minute more. Add sauce mixture. Stir until thickened, mix well and chill.

Wrapping: Follow direction for steamed barbecued pork buns on page 18.

Baking: Same as curry beef buns on page 45.

Do ahead notes: same as above.

Baked Ham Buns (For Tuey Bow)

Yield: 2 doz

Dough:
>1 recipe of the basic steamed barbecued pork bun (*pg. 18*)

Filling:
>1-4 oz can of sliced mushrooms
>2 cups finely diced ham
>2 stalks finely diced celery
>½ cup canned bamboo shoots, finely diced
>2 stalks green onions

Sauce mixture:
>2 tbsp cornstarch
>2 tbsp sherry
>2 tbsp light soy sauce
>1 tbsp vinegar
>1 tbsp sesame oil
>¼ cup chicken broth
>1 tsp *hoisin* sauce
>1 tsp oyster sauce

To make filling: Stir fry filling ingredients together for 2 minutes, then add sauce mixture. Stir until thickened. Chill well before wrapping.

Wrapping: Following direction for steamed barbecued pork buns on page 18.

Baking: Same as curry beef buns on page 45.

Do ahead notes: same as above.

Thick Rice Soup (Joak)

Deep Fried Devils (Yao Ja Guai)

Pork Lo Mein (Gee Yoke Lo Mein)

Don Don Noodles (Don Don Mein)

Yee Foo Wor Wonton

Tomato Beef Chow Mein

Noodles are a staple of the Chinese people. Every time I turn around, every restaurant I go to, somebody is eating noodles! Morning, noon and night, or any time in between, it's wontons, noodles, chowmein, chow fun, etc. Tell me, can you walk into any Italian restaurant at 10 in the morning or two a.m. and order spaghetti? Well, you can order it, but most likely you won't get it. Yet noodles dishes are available any time a Chinese restaurant is open. That can only mean one thing: We're noodle freaks!!

I remember that, when I was a child living in Hong Kong, there was a noodle and *joak* stand right outside our apartment. The aroma alone drove me bananas every morning. Unfortunately, my mom at that time was gung ho on western nutrition, which meant I had to have eggs, toast and warm milk for breakfast. UGH! It was sheer torture. While I was toying with the eggs and milk, my cousins, who were living with us at that time, would be gobbling bowls of delicious noodles or joak right in front of me!

One day I accidentally spilled my glass of milk and, since there wasn't any more, my mom let me have a bowl of joak. Ahhh . . . I became the most "accident prone" kid you've ever seen. It got so I was nicknamed "Jelly Fingers." To me, "Breakfast without noodles is a day without sunshine." Where have I heard that before?

Beef Chow Fun
(Gnow Yoke Chow Fun)

Yield: Serves 2-3

> 1 lb fresh rice noodles or 1 recipe of rice noodle
>   dough *(pg. 10)*
> ½ lb flank steak

Meat marinade:
> 2 tsp cornstarch
> 1 tsp sherry
> 2 tsp light soy sauce

> 1 lb green beans (or broccoli)
> 1 stalk green onion
> 2 cloves garlic, crushed
> 1 chunk ginger, crushed (size of a quarter)
> 4-5 tbsp oil
> 3 tbsp oyster sauce
> 2 tsp sesame oil
> 2 tsp light soy sauce

牛
肉
炒
粉

Preparation: Slice flank steak across the grain in thin strips no more than ⅛ inch thick. Mix with meat marinade for ½ hour. String and cut grean beans in 1½ inch length. Cut green onions the same length. Combine sauce mixture. Separate store bought rice noodles so they will not stick to each other. If you make your own noodles, cut them in ½ inch wide strips and separate them.

Cooking: Stir fry green beans in 1 tbsp. oil for 3-4 minutes, adding 2 tbsp. water the last 2 minutes and cover. Set aside. Add 1 tbsp. oil and brown the garlic and ginger. Stir fry beef, drizzle 1 tbsp. of oyster sauce on top. Set aside. Add 2 tbsp. oil and stir fry noodles, turning and adding a little water so they'll soften. It takes about 3-4 minutes. You may find you have to add more water or oil to keep a steady stream of steam to help soften the noodles. Add back the vegetables and meat. Add the rest of the oyster sauce, soy sauce and sesame oil.

Do ahead notes: Do through preparation.

Comments: Rice noodles can be purchased in Chinatown by the pound. They come in sheets or pre cut. You can easily make your own rice noodles; see page 10.

Tomato Beef Chowmein

Yield: 4 servings

牛肉炒麵

½ to ¾ lb flank steak

Meat marinade:
    2 tsp cornstarch
    2 tsp light soy sauce
    1 tbsp sherry

1 small onion, cut into thin wedges
2 stalks celery, cut into thin slices
2 medium tomatoes, cut into small wedges
1 tbsp brown sugar
¾ tsp salt

Sauce mixture:
    1 tbsp cornstarch
    4 tbsp catsup
    ¾ cup chicken broth
    1 tbsp oyster sauce

3 tbsp oil
¾ lb egg noodles *(see recipe on page 9)*

Preparation: Parboil noodles for 3 minutes. Rinse with cold water and drain well. Line cookie sheet with foil and rub with 1 tbsp. oil. Put boiled noodles in a thin layer on a cookie sheet. Place in a preheated 400° oven for 20 minutes. Turn over and brown for 10 more minutes (The noodles will stick together in a sheet.) Cool. Break into small pieces. Slice flank steak cross grain and mix with marinade for ½ hour. Mix sauce. Sprinkle brown sugar over tomato wedges.

Cooking: Heat wok. Add 1 tbsp oil and stir fry onions with celery for 1½ minutes, sprinkle a little salt and sugar to taste. Set aside. Heat 2 tbsp. oil, stir fry beef until almost done; add tomato wedges to heat through. Set aside. Stir in sauce mixture and wait for it to thicken. Add noodles and mix until they are soft. Add salt, vegetables and meat. Mix well and serve.

Do ahead notes: Make ahead and reheat in wok by stir frying, or place noodles in a loosely covered casserole in slow oven (250°) for ½ hour. Make sure food is at room temperature before reheating.

Comments: This is just one of many ways we make chowmein. In my earlier book, the *Chinese Village Cookbook*, I've shown how to make barbecue pork chowmein plus many other noodle dishes which are not repeated in this book. If you like noodles, do get a copy. I know you'll enjoy using the recipes and eating the results!

Pork Lo Mein (Gee Yoke Lo Mein)

Yield: 6-8 servings

½ lb fresh pork butt

Meat marinade:
    2 tsp cornstarch
    1 tsp sugar
    1 tbsp light soy sauce
    1 tsp sherry

2 tbsp fresh ginger, cut into thin slivers
4 dried mushrooms
½ cup bamboo shoots
1 red bell pepper
1 small onion, cut in small wedges
2 green onions, shredded and cut into 1-inch
    lengths
1 medium zucchini

Sauce mixture:
  4 tsp cornstarch
  1 cup chicken broth
  2 tbsp oyster sauce

  2 cloves garlic, crushed
  1 chunk of ginger, crushed, size of a quarter
  4 tbsp oil
  1 lb fresh egg noodles *(pg. 9)*

Seasonings for the noodles:
  2 tbsp oil
  1 tbsp sesame oil
  2 tbsp oyster sauce
  1½ tbsp light soy sauce
  1½ tsp vinegar

Preparation: Cut pork into thin, match stick sized strips. Mix with meat marinade and let stand for ½ hour. Soak mushrooms until soft. Discard stems and slice caps, bamboo shoots, red bell peppers and zucchini into thin strips. Mix sauce. Parboil noodles for 3 minutes. Rinse and drain. Bring another pot of water to boil and keep hot.

Cooking: Heat 2 tbsp. oil in wok and stir fry all the vegetables together for 2-3 minutes; sprinkle on a little salt and 1 tsp. of sugar. Set aside. Add 2 tbsp. oil and stir fry pork until done. Add sauce mixture, stir until thickened; add the vegetables. Stir until well mixed and keep warm.

Put noodles into the hot pot of water for 10-15 seconds, just to heat. Drain but do not rinse. Put noodles back in pot and add the noodle seasonings, tossing and mixing well. Transfer noodles to a big serving platter. Pour meat and vegetable mixture over noodles and serve.

Do ahead notes: Do through preparation

Comments: Do you notice the striking similarity between *lo mein* and Italian spaghetti? They are both egg noodles served with a meat sauce mixture over it. Wait 'til you taste this dish. Beware. It will spoil you forever for any other lo mein!

Mother's Favorite

This next recipe was one of my mother's favorite noodle snacks prepared by her family's chef when she was a young girl in Canton, China.

My grandfather was a very successful businessman and his estate encompassed several city blocks with a creek running through it. He had three concubines and there were approximately 50 people in the entire family, spanning several generations. They employed both a northern chef and a Cantonese one.

Girls at that time were encouraged to be feminine and to concern themselves with music, sewing, embroidery, etc. But my mother was a real tomboy at heart and, as far as my grandmother was concerned, a total disaster. She participated in all high school sports and joined the school ping pong club, where she became top player, leading her team to two city championships! In addition, she was the president of the hiking club and a member of the girls basketball team.

All these activities threw my grandmother into terrible fits! My mother bringing home a trophy meant another coughing spell for my grandmother. She would have loved to have picked up my mother and given her a good shellacking except, with, all due respect, have you ever seen a short, chubby, old Chinese lady running around with three inch feet? Yes, my grandmother had bound feet (it was fashionable in her day). Most of the time, she tottled around like a Chinese olive seed (pointed ends with a wide and round middle). Run? Forget it, you would have better luck pulling an elephant up a tree! It was a good thing she never found out my mother was learning cooking from the family chefs. (Cooking was considered a menial chore and girls from good families were not allowed to set foot in the kitchen.) Grandmother surely would have been the first human to go up into space!

Don Don Noodles (Don Don Mein)

Yield: 2-3 servings

½ lb egg noodles *(see recipe on page 9)*
½ cup fresh ground pork
2 tsp bean sauce

Sauce mixture:
½ to 1 tsp chili paste with garlic
2-3 tsp chopped green onion
2 tsp finely minced Szechwan turnip
  (*ja-choy*)
½ tsp finely minced ginger
1 tsp sesame oil
¼ cup chicken broth
1 tsp sherry

1 tsp oil

担
担
麵

Preparation: Parboil noodles for 3 minutes. Rinse with cold water and drain. Combine sauce mixture.

Cooking: Heat oil in wok and stir fry ground pork with bean sauce until done. Add sauce and mix until heated through. Add noodles, toss to mix well and serve.

Do ahead notes: Do through preparation. You may also cook the sauce in advance. Before serving, heat sauce with meat and add noodles to heat through.

Comments: This is a favorite Szechwan home-style noodle dish. If you prefer, you may delete the pork or add a small cake of canned *tofu* which has been finely diced. (Canned tofu is firmer and can withstand fine mincing without falling apart.)

Chili paste with garlic comes in a glass jar and can be purchased in shops specializing in oriental foods. You can substitute the flavor by crushing 1 or 2 dried red chili peppers plus 2 cloves of crushed garlic and browning them in 2 tbsp. oil until garlic turns brown. Discard garlic and chili and add 2 tsp. catsup to the oil. Use this mixture and stir fry the pork.

You must try this dish if you like noodles. It is absolutely sensational!

Yee Foo Wor Wonton

伊
府
雲
吞

Yield: 4 servings:

30 deep fried wontons *(page 13)*
2 cups *bok choy,* sliced
½ cup fresh pork butt, thinly sliced
½ cup chicken breast, thinly sliced

Meat marinade:
1 tbsp light soy sauce
1 tsp sesame oil
1 tsp sherry

½ cup canned abalone, thinly sliced
4 medium sized prawns, cleaned, shelled &
  de veined
1 stalk green onion, minced
1 quart chicken broth

Preparation: Mix sliced pork and chicken with meat marinade for ½ hour.

Cooking: Bring chicken broth to a boil. Add pork, chicken, *bok choy* and cook for 1 minute. Add prawns and fried wontons, cook until wontons are heated through. Add abalone and green onion last and heat for ½ minute more. Serve.

Do ahead notes: Do through preparation.

Comments: This is a slightly different version of the more familiar wonton soup. Here, the wontons are deep fried first then put into the broth, which makes the wonton wrappers produce a most interesting texture and flavor. Of course, if you want to make wonton soup, just drop the wrapped wontons into the broth. But you owe it to your curiosity to give this recipe a try.

Thick Rice Soup (Joak)

Yield: Serves 4 to 8

½ cup long grained rice 粥
½ cup glutinous rice
5 quarts chicken broth
1 lb ground pork
1 tbsp dark soy sauce
1 tsp salt
2 stalks green onions
12 water chestnuts

Condiments:
Sesame oil
White pepper
2-3 green onions, finely chopped
1 bunch Chinese parsley *(cilentro)*, fincly chopped
½ cup tea melon (sweet cucumber), finely chopped
½ cup Szechwan turnip (*ja choy*), finely chopped
½ cup chopped peanuts
10-12 deep fried devils *(see next recipe)*

Preparation: Rinse rice 2 or 3 times. Soak overnight. Mince green onions and water chestnuts. Mix with ground pork, soy sauce and salt.

Cooking: Bring stock and rice to a boil. Turn heat down and simmer for 2-3 hours or until the rice breaks down completely and the soup becomes thick and creamy. Turn heat up and add ground pork mixture, shaping 1 tsp. at a time into a small ball and dropping it into the soup. Cook for 5 minutes or until pork balls are done. Correct seasoning. Serve in individual soup bowls. Pass the condiments around for each person to choose his favorite toppings.

Do ahead notes: Make ahead and reheat slowly.

Comments: You can also use chicken slices, ground beef, fish filet or ham slices. A roast chicken or turkey carcass is excellent for making the stock. Just cook the carcass, rice and water together. Take out the carcass when the soup is done.

Deep Fried Devils (Yao Ja Guai)

油
炸
鬼

Yield: 24 or more small fried bread sticks

1 loaf frozen bread dough

Preparation: Thaw frozen bread dough overnight in refrigerator. In the morning, break bread dough into small pieces and roll out in long sausage like strips. Let sit at room temperature for 1 hour.

Cooking: Heat oil for deep frying. When oil is ready, take each strip of bread and pull on both ends just before dropping it into the hot oil. Deep fry until golden brown. Drain on paper towel and cut into 1 inch pieces. Use as a condiment for the *joak* (see previous recipe).

Do ahead notes: Do ahead early in the day. Fried bread sticks need not be hot when served.

Comments: When you serve Deep Fried Devils with joak, just put a few into the bowl of joak and let them soften a little before eating. They are devilishly good!

Bean Sauce Noodles (Ja Jeung Mein)

Yield: Serves 2-3

½ lb egg noodles *(see recipe on page 9)*
½ lb ground pork
1 cup shredded cucumber
2-3 tbsp bean sauce
2-3 cloves garlic, minced
¼ tsp white pepper
¼ tsp salt
½ tsp sugar
2 tbsp chicken broth or water
1 tbsp oil

Preparation: Parboil noodles in a pot of water with 3 tbsp. oil for 3 minutes. Rinse under cold water and drain well.

Cooking: In wok, heat 1 tbsp. oil. Brown pork with minced garlic and bean sauce until pork is done. Add remainder of seasonings and water. Mix well. Divide noodles into 2 or 3 portions according to appetite. Place in soup bowl. Spoon pork mixture on one side of the noodles and garnish the other side with the shredded cucumber. Serve.

Do ahead notes: Do through cooking of the pork mixture. Before serving, reheat mixture and spoon over cold noodles.

Comments: This is a very popular northern dish in which the noodles are served chilled. If you like yours hot (flavor wise), add ½-1 tsp. chili oil when you stir fry and you'll become a fire breathing dragon!

SWEET TREATS

In the realm of Chinese cooking, dessert is a neglected subject, probably because we Chinese, in general, do not place much emphasis (if any) on it. At the end of most dinners and banquets, we are content with simply sipping tea. Thoughts of eating sweets rarely engage us. Fortune cookies, long associated with Chinese food, are a Chinese American invention. Chinese, when visiting relatives in Hong Kong, bring fortune cookies as an American souvenier! How does that grab you?

Although lacking in quantity, we certainly make up for it in quality. Most of the following sweet treats are delicious, very light and not too sweet. They are perfect as a refreshing finale for lunch or dinner, although most Chinese prefer to snack on them between meals.

Most of them are associated in one way or another with festival celebrations, several of which I am saving for the next chapter in order to tell you more of their history and folklore.

Butterfly Cookies (Jow Wu Deep)

  Yield: About 80

1 pkg wonton wrappers *(see recipe on page 10)*
1 cup powdered sugar
oil for deep frying

Preparation: Cut each wonton wrapper into 2 rectangles. Lay 1 rectangle on top of the other to form a double thickness. Make 3 ½ inch slits in the center, lengthwise. To form a bow, pull 1 end through the middle slit.

Cooking: Deep fry butterflies until golden, about 1 minute or less. Drain on paper towel. Sift powdered sugar over both sides. Cool.

Do-ahead notes: These keep for 1 week in air tight containers.

Comments: Enlist the help of your children in making this and the Sweet Crescent recipe. Also, if you participate in scouting activities, these make fun cooking projects for the group.

Sweet Crescents (Teem Gok)

Yield: 7-8 doz.

  ½ cup chopped, salted cocktail peanuts
½ cup coconut flakes
½ cup brown sugar
½ cup granulated sugar
1 pkg wonton wrappers *(see recipe on page 10)*
1 egg, beaten

Preparation: Mix peanuts, coconut, brown and granulated sugar. Fold wonton squares into triangles. Round off the top corner with scissors. Place 1 tsp. filling in center. Moisten edges with beaten egg and seal.

Cooking: Deep fry in hot oil until golden, turning once. Drain. Cool. Store in air tight container.

Do ahead notes: These will keep for 3-4 weeks in an air tight container, although you probably won't have any left after the first day!

Comments: This sweet snack is found only in the southern part of China. It is a favorite snack during the Chinese New Year's celebration. You can also add chopped dry fruits to the fillings. They go well with ice cream or sherbet.

Custard Tarts (Don Tot)

Yield: 2 doz

蛋
撻

Tart pastry:
  ¼ cup butter
  ¼ cup lard
  1 egg
  6 tbsp sugar
  2 cups sifted all purpose flour

To make pastry: Cream butter with lard. Add egg and sugar. Beat well. Add flour, 1 cup at a time. The dough will be mealy. Work quickly with your hands to gather dough into a ball. Knead lightly so the mixture adheres. You may chill it at this point while making the filling.

Filling:
  2 whole extra large eggs
  3 extra large egg yolks
  1 cup whole milk
  ½ cup half and half
  1 cup sugar

To make filling: Be sure all ingredients are at room temperature. Beat whole eggs with egg yolks well. Beat at low speed. (Do not over beat.) Add sugar, then milk, half and half. Let mixture rest for 10-15 minutes. Skim off *all* the foam from mixture.

Assembling: Separate dough into 24 balls. Press each into a 2½ inch (measured across top) tart shell to an even layer across the bottom and all the way up the side. Fill tart shell with filling almost to the top.

Baking: Preheat oven at 300°. Place tarts on cookie sheet and bake for 45 minutes. Cool for 10-15 minutes. Loosen slightly by inserting a toothpick along the sides. The tart shell will unmold easily.

Do ahead notes: Custards can be made no more than ½ day ahead.

Comments: It is important that the ingredients for the filling be at room temperature and beaten over a warm bowl of water. Cold ingredients will cause filling to separate during baking. By skimming off the foam from the custard filling after beating, the custard will have a golden, creamy appearance with a velvety smooth texture, a most unique and delightful gastronomic treat! Do not bake on high heat; this would cause the custard to bubble up like a balloon and later collapse. Each oven is different, so you'll have to try a batch to find out what works for you. The crust should be a light beige to golden on the side and slightly more tan on the bottom side. There should be no browning at all of the custard.

Custard Tarts (Don Tot)

Sesame Cookies (Gee Ma Bang)

Yield: 10 doz

½ cup granulated sugar
½ cup brown sugar
1 egg
½ lb lard, no substitute
½ tsp almond extract
2 cups flour
½ tsp baking soda
¾ tsp baking powder
sesame seeds

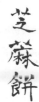

Preparation: Sift flour with baking soda and baking powder. Cream egg and lard together. Add sugars, then almond extract. Gradually add the dry ingredients and mix well. Chill for several hours before

59

handling. Roll 1 tsp. dough in your hands to form a ball. Then roll in sesame seeds, coating all sides.

Cooking: Place sesame balls about ¾ inches apart on cookie sheets. Bake in pre-heated 350° oven for 8-10 minutes. Cool.

Do ahead notes: These keep for weeks in air tight containers.

Comments: The recipe for Almond Cookies is basically the same. Roll 1 tbsp. dough to make the ball, then press an almond in the middle. Brush with beaten egg yolk and bake 8-10 minutes.

Steamed Sponge Cake (Gai Don Go)

鷄蛋糕

Yield: 1 7 inch square or 1 9 inch round cake

    5 extra large eggs at room temperature
    1 tbsp water
    1 cup sugar
    1 cup Swansdown cake flour (no substitute)
    1 tbsp melted butter

Preparation: Beat eggs, water and sugar for 10 minutes at high speed or for 20 minutes by hand. The color should turn almost vanilla and the consistency should become thick and creamy. Fold in flour, then melted butter. Line bottom of a 9 inch round or 7 inch square baking pan with cooking parchment paper. Pour batter into pan.

Cooking: Have water boiling in wok. Set cake pan on the steaming rack and cover. Steam 20 minutes at medium heat. Insert toothpick to see if done. Turn cake out and peel off paper. Serve warm or cold.

Do ahead notes: Cake can be stored for 2-3 days in a cake keeper.

Comments: Since this cake is served without any frosting or topping, it's appealing to those who don't like too sweet desserts. The texture is fine and firm but not hard. When pressed down, the cake springs back like a sponge.

Garnish with chilled fruits and pour some syrup from canned lichee over gelatin mixture. Serve.

Do ahead notes: Assemble dessert early in the day but do not garnish with marachino cherries until just before serving, as their color bleeds. That's the reason for rinsing them several times.

Chinese Pillows (Ning Moan Gok)

Yield: 2 doz.

48 wonton skins *(see recipe on page 10)*
¾ cup plum sauce
¾ cup lemon sauce
1 egg, beaten
oil for deep frying
1 cup powdered sugar

檸檬角

Wrapping: Drop 1 tsp. lemon or plum sauce in middle of wonton skin. Moisten edges with beaten egg. Place another wonton skin on top and press edges to seal.

Cooking: Deep fry in wok over medium-high heat until lightly golden. Drain on paper towels. Sift powdered sugar on both sides. Cool slightly before serving.

Do ahead notes: Wrap in advance. Deep fry just before serving. Pillows turn golden in less than 1 minute.

Comments: In Mexican cooking, there is a bread which is deep fried called *sopaipillas*. It is made with a baking powder dough but without filling and puffs up just like little pillows, too. Then sopaipillas are broken open and served with honey and butter. *Ning Moan Gok* is my Chinese version. You can also fill them with home made jams and jelly.

Almond Float (Hung Yun Lichee)

Yield: 8 servings

2 pkg. unflavored gelatin
1¾ cups cold water
6 tbsp granulated sugar
1½ cup milk
1 tbsp almond extract
1-6½ oz can mandarin oranges
1-1 lb can lichee nuts
10-12 marachino cherries

杏仁荔枝

Preparation: Dissolve gelatin in ½ cup cold water with the sugar. Stir until well mixed. Meanwhile, bring rest of water (1¼ cup) to a boil and pour over the gelatin mixture. Stir until mixture is clear. Add milk and almond extract. Pour into a 7½ inch×12 inch pan. Refrigerate until set. Chill fruits. Rinse marachino cherries.

Assembling: Cut almond jello into ¾ inch squares. Lift out carefully into individual dessert glasses.

FESTIVALS & LEGENDS

The Good Luck Charm

Jeen Duey is a deep fried sweet dumpling the size of a small tangerine with either a sweet bean paste filling or coconut and peanut filling that are served during the Chinese New Year. One of the many folklores associated with jeen duey is that, since it resembles a small tangerine, which is pronounced "gut" in Chinese, and, phonetically, "gut" also means luck, jeen duey has become symbolically associated with luck. That's one reason why it is a traditional New Year's sweet treat we share with our family and friends.

Sesame Seed Puffs (Jeen Duey)

Yield: 3 doz

Dough:
    1 recipe of the sweet glutinous rice dough
       (*pg. 11*)

Filling:
    1 recipe of the sweet crescent filling (*pg. 57*).
       or
    2 cups canned red bean paste (*Dow-suh*)

Sesame seeds
Oil for deep frying

Wrapping: Divide dough in half and separate each half into 12 portions. Roll each to form a ball. Flatten by hand to a 3 inch round. Put 1 teaspoon of red bean paste or sweet crescent filling in center, press opposite sides together to seal. Roll again in palms to form a round ball. Roll ball in sesame seeds. Repeat with rest of the dough.

Cooking: Heat oil in wok over medium heat (350° in a deep fryer). Deep fry four balls per batch, moving them constantly so they do not stay at the bottom. After 2-3 minutes, balls will start to float. Rotate them with chopsticks or a slotted spoon, gently pushing them against the side of the wok. (This action will help the balls retain a rounder shape). Continue frying them until the balls attain a medium golden brown color. (Approximately 8-10 minutes.) Drain on paper towel and cool for 5 minutes before serving.

Do ahead notes: Jeen Dueys can be made ahead and kept refrigerated for several days. Reheat by deep frying or in oven at 350° for 10 minutes.

The Journey Of Forty Nine Days

Although the Chinese people are extremely superstitious, the word "death" is frequently used in many idiomatic expressions, sometimes cropping up in forms of swear words. I'm no philosopher, but my feelings are that we look at death as an antecedent to birth. (Many Chinese believe in re incarnation and I have a story about that too.) Therefore, death is as natural as eating, breathing, sleeping, etc. In many families, you can find coffins for each family member stored away in the attic.

Once I took a long trip with my mother (about 1 month's time on foot) to visit her sister. One night we stayed at the house of some friends. Mother was up playing *mah jong* and I was sent to bed. (The people made up extra bedding in the spare room.) Just before I dozed off, I happened to look up and there in the loft were four coffins all lined up neatly in a row! I was only about eight or nine at that time, and I didn't know whether or not those coffins were empty or full! My legs turned rubbery and I couldn't even get out of bed! I threw the cover over myself, even though it was in the middle of a hot summer night. My heart was pounding so fast and furiously I thought it would jump out of my throat! I kept hearing creaking noises and, of course, I expected that any minute the coffins would all open up and . . . . AGH! I must have lost 10 pounds that night just through perspiration alone! It wasn't until the next day that I found out it was customary in many parts of China (Thank God, not in my family or my village!) that people purchase coffins whenever they could afford it, in order to prepare for that inevitable final journey!

In my village, when a death occured in the family, the deceased lay in state (usually in the living room) until it was time for the burial. The burial date was selected by an astrologer to harmonize with the deceased's birth sign, etc. Needless to say, the sooner the better, especially in the summer months!

If the deceased was wealthy, his family members would place pieces of carved jade in all body openings so that evil spirits could not enter. It was also thought that jade could retard body decomposition. Some wealthy families even put a genuine pearl on the deceased's lips so when he arrived at the pearly gate, he could bribe the gate keeper for fast entry!

On the day of the funeral, the elder son would lead family members to the open coffin to pay final respect. When that was accomplished, the undertaker closed the coffin while everyone looked the other way.

If you so much as sneaked a glance, it was believed your soul would be stolen and trapped inside the coffin. The undertaker was the *only one* who could look (he had special powers to protect himself.). I've often wondered if the undertaker made up that rule so he could go shopping for the family jewels! Come to think of it, they were all pretty well off. Hmmmmm . . . . .

The funeral procession is a very solemn and important occasion to the Chinese, for we believe in giving the deceased a grand and final send off to show our proper respect. In cities, the procession would be accompanied by several groups of marching bands playing very slow and mournful music. Professional mourners would be hired to give additional vocal wailing which was considered a very necessary part of the show. Flowers by the truck load would accompany the family to the graveside.

In our village, things were much simpler. The mourners wore traditional white headbands and sacks, white being the color of mourning. In large families, different color arm bands denoted different generations. Every mourner wailed as loudly as possible during the procession. Usually several local musicians played very sad tunes on wind instruments.

Once at the graveside, the family would burn incense, candles and paper images representing all the human comforts the deceased would need for his long journey to the other world. Images of things such as household furnishings, clothing, servants, animals and paper money were common. We also brought food along. A bowl of rice with chopsticks standing up in the middle instead of placed along the side was left at the graveside.

The journey, according to our beliefs, takes 49 days to complete so, every seven days, we visited the graveside to offer more food and burn more paper images and incense, to make sure the deceased enjoyed a pleasant journey.

Thereafter, on the third day of the third month each year, we celebrated *Ching Ming*, a private family observance that pays respect to our ancestor's graves. In China, our family plot is located in the hills behind the village. We would again bring food and paper offerings. One of the festival dishes was this nine layer pudding, a most delicious sweet treat any time of the year.

9 Layer Pudding (Gow Chung Go)

Yield: 1 9 inch round pudding

2½ cups tapioca starch (no sifting)
2½ cups brown sugar (packed tightly)
2½ cups water
2½ tbsp oil
1-2 tbsp sesame seeds

九層糕

Preparation: Bring sugar and water to a boil. Stir to completely dissolve sugar. Let stand until cool. In a mixing bowl, combine tapioca starch with sugared water until smooth. Add oil and mix again.

Cooking: Start water in steamer. When it comes to a boil, ladle ⅓ cup batter into a generously greased 9 inch pie pan. Steam for 5 minutes and add another ⅓ cup batter on top. Steam another 5 minutes and repeat process 9 times altogether. Take pudding out and sprinkle sesame seeds on top. Let pudding set for 24 hours before cutting.

Do ahead notes: Since this pudding requires 24 hours to set, it is a great make ahead item.

Comments: Be sure to wipe off the inside of the cover each time you add batter so the water will not drip into the pudding. The pudding is *very* sticky right after steaming. Don't even bother with it for at least 24 hours. When ready to serve, invert cake upside down on wax paper and turn right side up again. Cut with sharp cleaver or knife into diamond shapes and arrange in a sun burst or star like pattern on a serving platter. I love to snack on them or have them with hot tea. The soft and chewy texture contrasts pleasantly with the nut like flavor and texture of the sesame seeds. This translucent pudding tastes like a chewy piece of Jello or Chinese jellied candy. No wonder it is one of the all-time favorites among many Chinese.

The Lucky Numbers

But why nine layers?

One aspect of the Chinese culture places a great deal of emphasis on numbers. We believe numbers carry a special kind of significance. For instance, number 2 is a happy number. The Chinese character "happiness" appears twice in a Chinese wedding invitation.

Another lucky number is 9, for we believe it is related to heavenly power. Almost all pagodas in China have nine tiers. Most banquets consists of nine courses. There are nine species of the Chinese dragon, the symbol of royalty, power and everlasting life. Each dragon possesses nine characteristics or likenesses, one from each of the species. Because of all the special significant power related to the number nine, it is our hope that the 9 Layer Pudding will help the deceased spirit in his quest to ascend to heaven.

The Mongoloid Spot

Of course, not everybody gets to go to heaven. Many Chinese believe the majority of us will reincarnate into another life back on earth. How is this accomplished? Listen . . . .

All oriental babies are born with a black and blue spot(s) on their buttocks or sometimes their backs. They are known as Mongoloid spots and, as far as I know, there is no medical explanation for them. Ah . . . but how about a non medical explanation? This little tale was told to me by my grandmother and I think you'll love it as much as I enjoy sharing it!

As I mentioned earlier, we burn paper images for our deceased. This includes paper money. Now, Chinese paper money is printed in such a way that, on one side, it is negotiable in heaven (there is a picture of *Yoke Wong,* the jade emperor of heaven); the other side is good "down below" (it shows the picture of our God of Hell). We think of everything, don't we? Why?

Since many of us will be reincarnated, it stands to reason that very few go straight to heaven. The rest of the gang must go "the other way" and pay for all the sins committed. After *Seung Doe Sahn* and *Lok Yau Wok,* which means "climbing mountains studded with blades and being deep fried in hot oil" (among other fun and games in the devil's amusement park), you are finally brought before *Yuan Lau Wong,* the God of Hell. He alone decides what your next life will be. Depending on how you behaved in the previous life, theoretically, you can be reincarnated into an insect, reptile, bird, animal or human. Once judgment is pronounced, you swim across the river of life to the other side. You must drink water from the river of life, for it makes you forget all memories of the life you have just left.

When you get to the other side, you crawl through the tunnel of birth. This tunnel is very narrow and low so you must get on all fours in order to fit yourself through. To help you to get through quickly, a fellow with a big paddle is stationed at the mouth of the tunnel. He gives you a big swat in the behind to get you in and, voilà! Zare ees zee spot in zee derrière! Can you imagine a 500 pound lady trying to get through?! Ouch! Think of the traffic jam she causes! Maybe that's why you seldom see fat Chinese. We don't wanna get them spankings!

Festival Of Winter Solace

The Chinese welcome in the winter season (*guaw doan*) on the longest day of the year by having a family reunion with all the living members paying respects to the deceased. But instead of going to the graveside, this is a much happier occasion. Like the American Thanksgiving celebration, we give thanks for the good harvest and invite our deceased ancestors to share the family's good fortune. The following White Turnip Pudding Cake (*Lo Bok Go*) has always been the traditional offering at this time. Like so many other festival dishes, it has become another favorite dim sum item among "tea goers."

White Turnip Pudding Cake (Lo Bok Go) 蘿白糕

Yield: 1 9 inch round cake

2½ cups diced Chinese turnip (*lo bok*) or Japanese *daikon*
2¼ cups chicken broth
4 tbsp oil
⅓ cup dried shrimp
1 cup barbecued pork or cooked ham
2 tbsp salted turnip (*choan choy*), minced
1 tsp salt
½ cup green onions, chopped
½ cup Chinese parsley (*cilentro*), chopped
2 cups Swansdown cake flour (no substitute)

Preparation: Soak dried shrimp for 1 hour, then finely dice after draining. Bring diced turnips, 2 tbsp. oil and 1 cup chicken broth to a boil and simmer for 12-15 minutes or until turnip is soft. Do not drain liquid.

Heat wok and add 2 tbsp. oil and stir fry diced shrimp for 1 minute, then add diced pork, salted turnips, 1 tsp. salt and ⅓ cup each of the green onions and Chinese parsley. Set aside.

Mix 2 cups of Swansdown cake flour with 1¼ cup of chicken broth until smooth. Add stir fried mixture and the boiled turnip, including the remaining liquid in the pot. Mix well. Pour mixture into 9 inch cake pan.

Cooking: Set cake pan over steam rack in wok. Cover. Bring water to a boil and turn heat to simmer. Steam for ½ hour or longer until cake is set. Sprinkle remaining green onions and parsley over cake. Cool for at least ½ hour before cutting.

Do ahead notes: Can be made ahead and frozen. Reheat by thawing first, then cut in thin slices. Brown both sides in a little oil until outside is crunchy. Serve with light soy sauce mixed with a little hot sauce.

Comments: As you can see, Turnip Cake can be served in slices with or without browning, depending on personal preferences. In most tea houses, the cakes are pan fried before serving. However, in my house, they are eaten up before they ever get close to the skillet. That's how crazy we are for this delicious pudding cake!

The Moon Festival (Bot Yeut Jit)

There once was an emperor named Ming Huang who had a young and beautiful mistress named Yang Kwei Fei. Ming Huang, although a fairly good looking man, was nevertheless in his 60s. He knew that it would be just a matter of time before either his gorgeous mistress would get tired of him or

he'd become completely dissipated. Even though he was able to give her anything she wanted—money, position—(he even entrusted all the power of government to her brother), he was unable to give her the thing he knew she wanted the most—his youth.

Word reached him that within his kingdom, a magician had discovered an elixir to the fountain of youth. One swallow would immediately turn back the years and render the client immortal. Ming Huang was beside himself. He ordered the magician to give him a small bottle of the elixir and then had the fellow beheaded because he didn't want anyone else to have the magic potion. (Stupid! He just cooked his own goose.)

Meanwhile, Ming Huang's empress was sad and depressed because her husband no longer loved her. Although Ming Huang had had many other mistresses (If I'd been his wife, I would have sent the African pygmies after him!), she noticed that never before had he lost his heart so completely as he had to Yang Kwei Fei. She blamed it on her own advancing years. She too, wished to become young again; at least she would have a better chance of winning back her husband.

When the empress learned Ming Huang had the elixir in his possession, she searched his apartment high and low and found it. She was just about to leave when Ming Huang entered. Fearing he would discover the vile on her, she quickly swallowed it. The potion took effect immediately and she turned into a beautiful maiden. She flew off to the moon before Ming Huang could chop her head off.

Ming Huang was mad all right, but he also recognized that when a family member becomes immortal, it is definitely a good omen. He ordered national celebration of her immortality by having everyone prepare and eat the moon cake, a special round, flaky pastry with sweet fillings. The roundness of the pastry, of course, represents the shape of the full moon.

But things were not going well. An Lu Shan, a Tartar courtier, decided to take over the empire. He and his barbarians killed Ming Huang's mistress (she had told him to get lost when he made a pass at her) and her brother, forced Ming Huang into exile and plunged the country into many years of internal unrest under Tartar rule.

The Chinese, ever so resourceful, hatched a clever plot to overthrow the Tartars. Since the Tartars never had learned to read Chinese, it was decided that a written message could be placed inside moon cakes. (You are now witnessing the birth of the Chinese fortune cookies!). The message was to instruct everyone to kill any and all Tartars near by immediately upon reading the note. Since everyone celebrated the festival on the evening of August 15 when the moon was at its fullest, the cakes would be consumed at the same time. The plan worked and the Tartar rule was put to an end. Ming Huang was able to return to his throne and ruled for a short time before passing away.

Making the moon cake is a very difficult and complicated process, which I don't even know how to begin. We usually buy them from bakeries in Chinatown. But I have a fun little recipe I jokingly call The Mock Moon Cake which I think you'll enjoy trying.

Mock Moon Cake (Hoan Jo Bang)

Yield: 1 doz

 40 *jujube* nuts (Chinese red dates), about 1 cup chopped
1 cup sesame seeds
6 tbsp sugar
9 sheets *filo* dough

Preparation: Soak the whole dried *jujube* nuts in ½ cup water for 2 days. Take out seeds and put through blender with the soaked liquid and sugar. Add sesame seeds, mix well.

Wrapping: Cut *filo* dough lengthwise into 4½ inch wide strips. Stack strips on top of each other and cover with slightly damp cloth. Fold each strip into halves crosswise 3 times. Cut 2 folded strips into 4½ inch circles and the third strip into a 3 inch circle. Line buttered or greased muffin tins with the 4½ inch circles. Place filling in cup until ½ inch from top. Place the 3 inch circle of dough over the filling and seal edges with beaten egg. Brush top with oil. Bake at 350° for 20 minutes. Cool for 10 minutes. Cake should unmold easily especially if you use Teflon coated muffin tins. (Be sure to oil each strip separately before folding and cutting).

Do ahead notes: These delicious little cakes will keep for a week or more. Reheat by baking in a 300° oven for 10 minutes or until heated through. The crust will be light and flaky. Be sure to read page 32 on working with the filo dough before you begin making this recipe.

The Dragon Boat Festival

On the fifth day of the fifth moon, we celebrate the Dragon Boat Festival. This festival is considered a national holiday and, of course, has a famous legend which I am going to tell you.

Once there was a knight who was the emperor's favorite subject. He was a good man and very loyal to his emperor. However, the emperor's only son was extremely jealous of him. After months of planning, he successfully plotted and executed an elaborate scheme whereby the knight was accused of being a traitor (shades of a 1950 Hollywood movie script!).

Persons convicted of such treachery would normally have been executed, but the emperor, who dearly loved his friend, didn't have the heart to have him killed. Instead, he banished him from his kingdom. The knight, who couldn't bear the thought of living in exile, drowned himself in the river. (No fuss, no muss. Besides, his wife would have hated to have had to clean up the mess had he chosen to commit *hari kari*.)

That night, his spirit visited the emperor and told him of his innocence. The emperor, grieving the death of his beloved subject and friend, declared it a day of national mourning. And to see that the deceased spirit was well provided for and well fed, people were asked to throw food into the river. The food, call *joan*, is wrapped in *ti* leaves so it is water proof. Inside it has rice with either a sweet bean paste filling or a meat and nut filling.

Since it was believed there were evil spirits and monsters (Oh no, not that three headed juvenile again!) in the deep of the river, the emperor decorated fleets of boats with dragon like carvings and invited musicians to play different percussive instruments. The boats cruised up and down the river, chasing away the evil spirit and allowing his friend, the knight, to enjoy his meal.

The Chinese Village Rock Group

In many parts of China, there may not be a real live dragon boat race because of geography. I was fortunate to witness this colorful and exciting (and comical) race because our village is situated beside a river. Usually there was a competition among several nearby villages, all of them having access to the river.

The women, of course, spent days making the joan and many banners to decorate the boat. For at least two months prior to "D" day, the men would practice rowing for an hour prior to sundown. There were no trophies given; it was a matter of "honor" for the entire village to be the winner.

No banners decorated the boat until the day of the race, as it was not uncommon for some overly enthusiastic group from another village to steal them. Since we were all amateurs and we couldn't afford to hire any professional drummers, practically any volunteer was accepted and anything that made loud noises was loaded on board. I saw woks, large square kerosine cans, big hollow trunks of bamboo, an odd assortment of tin cans, bells and, the prize of them all, a beat up bugle. The din from the combined home made band would have given any present day rock group a run for its money!

Afterward, everybody gathered in the village square and had joan plus many other goodies. Boy! Did we stuff ourselves silly!

You don't have to have a dragon-boat race to enjoy these delicious Chinese tamales. The actual preparation and wrapping is not half as difficult as it sounds in the recipe. Besides, the tamales can be frozen once they are cooked. They are quite expensive when purchased from Chinatown and they generally are not half as good as those home made.

Chinese Tamales (Joan)

Yield: about 2½ to 3 doz

Rice mixture:
    5 lb glutinous rice
    2 tbsp salt
    2 tsp sugar
    1 tbsp oil

    1¼ tsp monosodium glutimate (optional)

½ lb dried shrimp
½ lb shelled chestnuts
½ lb shelled raw peanuts
6 pairs Chinese sausage
1½ lb ham or barbecued pork
2 doz salted eggs
1 bunch dried *ti* leaves

Preparation: Soak *ti* leaves for 2 days, change water each day. On the third day, boil leaves for 1 hour in a big pot of water with ½ cup vinegar and ½ cup salt. Rinse under hot water. (Cold water will cause the leaves to break.) Soak again in warm water for 2 more days. On the day of wrapping, dry ti leaves between towels. Keep the leaves damp so they'll remain pliable.

On the night before wrapping, soak chestnuts and rice. Next morning, soak dried shrimp for 1 hour. Drain everything. Combine rice mixture. Stir fry the raw peanuts, dried shrimp and chestnuts separately, each in ½ tsp. salt and 2 tbsp. oil. Set aside in separate dishes. Cut each sausage into 3 sections. Cut ham or barbecued pork in approximately the same shape. Crack open the salted eggs and discard the whites. Cut yolks in half. (The yolks have hardened during the salting process.)

Wrapping: Place 2 leaves one on top of the other, overlapping about 1 inch. Fold leaves in half crosswise. Now fold 1 inch lengthwise along 1 edge. Open the other edge and a pocket is formed. Hold this pocket in your cupped hand to give support. Insert a third leaf around the outside next to the other 2 leaves so the pocket becomes higher.

Spread a thin layer of rice on the bottom and sides of pocket (about ¼ to ⅓ cup, depending on the size of the leaves). Now put in a piece of sausage, ham or barbecued pork, halved egg yolk, several peanuts, dried shrimps and 1 or 2 chestnuts. Top with about the same amount of rice as before.

Lightly pack and shape fillings to enable you to fold the leaves together over the top. Now fold all the pointed ends of the leaves over the top. Tie with strings securely, butcher style. (First wind strings 7 or 8 times across then 2 or 3 times lengthwise.) Repeat wrapping procedure until all ingredients are used.

Cooking: Fill a large pot about half way up with water and add 2 tbsp. of boric acid powder. Bring water to a boil for 1 minute. Slowly add the wrapped tamales. Make sure the water completely covers the tamales. Bring back to a boil and simmer for 4-6 hours, depending on the size of the joan. Drain. Unwrap and serve hot. Use light soy sauce for dipping.

Do ahead notes: Cooked tamales freeze beautifully for several months. To reheat, bring frozen tamales to a boil in a pot of water and simmer for at least ½ hour.

Comments: It is unfortunate that few of my contemporaries know how to make joan. We have become too busy and too westernized to spend the time to learn some of these marvelous old recipes. I hope the inclusion of this and other traditional recipes in this book will rekindle old memories, sparkle new interest and wake up those sleeping taste buds.

DIM SUM MENUS

It is one thing to have tea lunch in a restaurant, where you can order as many different goodies as your heart desires (or your tummy permits), but quite another matter when you serve them at home. Now you are the cook and waitress and you alone have to do all the work. I thought it would be helpful to provide you several suggested menus to give you ideas. They can be served in a sit down or buffet style lunch.

These menus are put together with the following features in mind: 1) Each includes a main dish such as noodles (the first item listed on each menu) with several smaller dim sum dishes accompanying them. 2) These accompanying items are chosen to compliment the main dishes because they offer a balance of taste, texture and appearance. 3) Most are fix ahead items so you will only have minimum last minute work. 4) The menus are flexible enough so that you can serve 2 or 20 people by merely increasing or decreasing the amount in the recipes (such as the noodle dishes) or the number of dim sum in the smaller items. 5) Although it is not necessary, I am including at least 1 dessert item in each menu for those of you who have a sweet tooth. Enjoy!

MENU NO. 1

Tomato Beef Chowmein
Crispy Taro Turnover
Shrimp Bonnet
Stuffed Rice Noodle Rolls
Butterfly Cookies
Tea

This lovely menu allows you to make all of the items ahead of time. The only last minute work is reheating the Taro Turnovers.

One week before: Make and freeze Taro Turnovers and Shrimp Bonnets.

Day before: Make the noodles in the oven for Tomato Beef Chowmein. Cut and slice all meats and vegetables. Make the Rice Noodle Roll and the Butterfly Cookies. Defrost Shrimp Bonnets and Turnovers overnight.

Day of the luncheon: Make the Tomato Beef Chowmein an hour earlier and reheat according to directions. Reheat Shrimp Bonnets by steaming. Deep fry taro just before serving.

MENU NO. 2

Thick Rice Soup
Deep Fried Devils
Seafood Stuffed Peppers
Spring Rolls
Sesame Cookies
Tea

This is a very substantial lunch because the rice soup is very filling. I especially like to serve this in the colder months; the rice soup goes down nice and warm!

1 week before: Make Spring Rolls and freeze them.

Day before: Make the Rice Soup, Sesame Cookies and stuff the peppers but do not cook them yet. Thaw out frozen bread dough and Spring Rolls overnight in the refrigerator.

Day of the luncheon: Slowly reheat the Rice Soup for at least 1 hour or more. During this time, make the Deep Fried Devils and the sauce for the Stuffed Pepper and set aside. Just before serving, pan fry the Stuffed Peppers while you reheat the Spring Rolls by deep frying.

MENU NO. 3

Barbecued Pork Buns
White Turnip Pudding Cake
Shrimp Toast
Curried Chicken Wings
Sweet Rice Pudding Cake
Tea

Here's a menu for bread lovers. You don't have to restrict yourself to only 1 kind of filling. Sometimes I serve several kinds of buns for variety if I have a large crowd.

1 week before: Make and freeze the buns, Shrimp Toast and Turnip Cake.

Day before: Defrost buns and Turnip Cake. Make Curried Chicken Wings and Sweet Rice Pudding Cake.

Day of the luncheon: Reheat buns, Curried Chicken Wings and Shrimp Toast according to recipe directions. Slice the Turnip Cake. Just before serving, pan fry the Turnip Cake.

MENU NO. 4

Don Don Noodles
Steamed Pork Turnovers
Mini Chicken Rolls
Deep-Fried Wontons in Sweet and Sour Sauce
Steamed Sponge Cake
Tea

This is a very flexible menu, as you can substitute another type of noodle dish (such as the Bean Sauce Noodles) for the one above. The rest of the items are all fix aheads.

1 week before: Make and freeze Pork Turnovers, Deep Fried Wontons and the Sweet and Sour Sauce.

Day before: Make Steamed Sponge Cake and Mini Chicken Rolls. Dice all ingredients for the noodle dish. Defrost frozen items.

Day of the luncheon: Reheat wontons, sweet and sour sauce, Pork Turnovers and Mini Chicken Rolls according to directions. Just before serving, make the noodles while above items are reheating.

MENU NO. 5

Muu Shu Pork
Peking Doilies
Onion Pancakes
Pot Stickers
Almond Float
Tea

Here's a menu to delight northern Chinese food fans. Make sure you have plenty of hot chili oil, as well as soy and vinegar dips* for those who like their food spicy.

Week before: Make and freeze Peking Doilies, Onion Pancakes and wrap the Pot Stickers—but do not cook them.

Day before: Slice all ingredients for Muu Shu Pork and make the Almond Float. Defrost Peking Doilies and Onion Pancakes but not the Pot Stickers.

Day of luncheon: Stir fry filling for Muu Shu Pork and keep warm. Reheat the Peking Doilies and Onion Pancakes according to directions while you cook the Pot Stickers.

*4 tbsp. light soy sauce to 1 tbsp. white vinegar and 2 tsp. sesame oil.

MENU NO. 6

Beef Chow Fun
Deep Fried Pork Turnovers
Parchment Chicken
Shrimp Boat
Custard Tarts
Tea

The Chow Fun dish, be it with beef or barbecued pork, is an all time favorite lunch item among the Chinese. It is not surprising to find restaurants running out of rice noodles as early as 1 o'clock in the afternoon. You can be sure to receive rave comments whenever you serve this menu.

Week before: Make and freeze Deep Fried Pork Turnovers and Parchment Chicken.

Day before: Slice all ingredients for the noodle recipe. Make filling for the Shrimp Boats, rice noodles, (if store bought are not available) and the dough for the Custard Tarts. Defrost frozen items.

Day of luncheon: Make Custard Tarts early in the morning. Fill the Shrimp Boats. Reheat Pork Turnovers, Parchment Chicken, and steam the Shrimp Boats at the same time you make the beef rice noodles.

MENU NO. 7

Yee Foo Wor Wonton
Savory Pork Triangles
Pickled Mustard Greens
Steamed Rice Noodle Rolls
Chinese Pillows
Tea

Wonton in soup is another perennial favorite luncheon or midnight snack and most Chinese prefer it over the deep fried wontons. It is so filling and nourishing that I frequently serve this alone for lunch or dinner. Here, we have it as the featured item on the menu.

Week before: Deep fry the wontons and freeze. Make the Pickled Mustard Greens.

Day before: Make the Pork Triangles and the Rice Noodle Rolls. Slice all ingredients for the wonton soup. Defrost wontons.

Day of the luncheon: Wrap Chinese Pillows early and keep covered loosely. Reheat Pork Triangles and wontons according to directions. Deep fry the pillows while you finish making the Yee Foo Wor Wonton.

MENU NO. 8

Pork Lo Mein
Siu Mai
Curry Beef Buns
Beef Jerky
9 Layer Pudding Cake
Tea

Here's a menu for those who love noodles, like me. The *lo mein* to the Chinese is what *fettucini* is to Italians. The sauce in this recipe is tantalizingly delicious. All the other dim sum items are make aheads, so this is one of the easiest and tastiest menus to try.

Week before: Bake and freeze Curry Beef Buns. Make Siu Mai and freeze.

Day before: Make Beef Jerky and 9 Layer Pudding Cake (make sure you allow at least 24 hours setting time). Slice all ingredients for the noodle dish. Defrost Curry Beef Buns.

Day of the lunch: Reheat Siu Mai and Curry Beef Buns according to directions. While the above items are cooking, make the lo mein.

GLOSSARY OF INGREDIENTS:

Here is a list of ingredients common in Chinese cooking. For the sake of simplicity, the list includes only those ingredients used in this book. All of them can be purchased from stores specializing in Oriental foods although, with the increasing interest in Chinese cooking, some now are available in supermarkets.

ANISE, STAR: (see star anise).

BAMBOO SHOOTS: An ivory colored vegetable, usually available in cans, either whole or sliced. The unused portions can be kept for about 1 week in jars, provided you change the water each day to keep them from spoiling. (*Juk soon.*)

BEAN CAKE: Also called *tofu* or *dow fu*. Because it's made from soy beans, bean cake has a high protein content. It's an excellent food for babies, since it digests easily. It's also good for children who don't care for meat.

   Bean cake has a smooth, creamy texture and a bland taste, so it readily absorbs the flavor of soups and sauces. It can be purchased fresh in produce sections or is available in cans. Fresh bean cake spoils easily; it must be used within 1 or 2 days of purchase.

BEAN SAUCE: Also called brown bean sauce or soy bean condiment. The Chinese name is *mein see*. This is prepared from the residue left after making soy sauce. It has a thick consistency and is available in cans or jars. Bean sauce is used to flavor pork and fowl, in addition to bland vegetables or bean cakes. The unused portion will keep for months when stored in a jar in the refrigerator.

BEAN SPROUTS: A vegetable grown from green *mung* peas. It has a 2 inch long white shoot with a small green hood. The texture is delicate and crunchy. Bean sprouts shouldn't be cooked for more than 1 minute or they'll become limp and lose their crispness. Fresh bean sprouts don't keep well and should be used as soon as possible. (*Nga choy.*)

BLACK BEANS: The Chinese name is *dow see*. These are tiny, soft, extremely salty black beans. Used to season meat and seafood, they're first washed, then mashed with fresh garlic and ginger. They can be stored at room temperature.

BOK CHOY: A leafy vegetable with white stalks and dark-green leaves. It looks somewhat like Swiss chard but the taste isn't as strong. *Bok choy* can be stir fried alone or with meat and can be dropped into broth for soup.

CHINESE PARSLEY: Also known as *cilentro* or coriander. This is a bright green herb with slender, delicate stems and small, serrated flat leaves. Highly aromatic, it has a strong, pungent flavor and is used as a garnish or as a bouquet in roasting poultry. (*Yuen sai.*)

CHINESE CABBAGE: A tall, tightly packed vegetable with wide, white stalks and yellow green wrinkled leaves. It is delicious when cooked and is one vegetable that tastes better when a bit overcooked. It can be used for soup or stir fry dishes. (*Wong bok* or *yea choy*.)

CHINESE SAUSAGE: The Chinese name is *lop cheung*. These slender pork sausages come in pairs, each one 6 inches long. They're sliced thin and can be cooked directly on top of rice or steamed separately. Stir fry them with any vegetable or use in rice stuffings. To store, wrap in plastic bags and freeze.

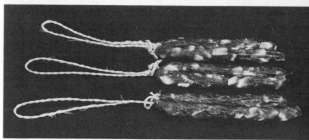

CHILI OIL: Red colored oil that is hot in flavor. To make your own, heat up 1 cup of oil and add ¼ to ⅓ cup dried red chilies and 1 tsp. of *achuete* for red coloring. If achuete is unavailable, use paprika. Let chili stand in oil for several days before draining. (*Lot yau*)

CHILI PASTE WITH GARLIC: This reddish, hot flavored paste comes in a jar. We use this to season our food. Just add a teaspoon or two to the stir fry at the last minute. (*Lot jiu jeung yau.*)

CILENTRO: See Chinese parsley.

CLOUD EAR FUNGUS: A small, dried, grayish brown fungus about 1 inch long. When soaked, it expands to several times its size. The texture is crunchy and delicate and it is either steamed or used in stir fried dishes. (*Wan yee.*)

CORIANDER: See Chinese parsley.

DOW FU: See bean cake.

EGG ROLL WRAPPERS: Made with flour, eggs and water, these can be purchased in Chinatown noodle factories or in the frozen food section of many supermarkets. They are easily made from scratch if a noodle making machine is available to you. Immediately rewrap the unused portion in plastic wrap and freeze. (*Chun guen pay.*)

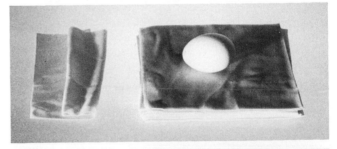

5 SPICE POWDER: A blend, in powder form, of star anise, cinnamon, cloves, fennel and anise pepper. It has a mustard color and is used in roasting meats and poultry. (*Eng hung fun.*)

GINGER, FRESH ROOT: A gnarled, spicy, beige colored root. It's a must in Chinese cooking. Never substitute ginger powder. In fact, it's better to leave ginger out completely if you don't have the root on hand. It's especially good to use ginger on seafood since it alleviates the fishy odor. It will keep for months frozen or, break it into small chunks and store in a refrigerated jar filled with sherry. Wait 'til you taste that sherry! (*Geung.*)

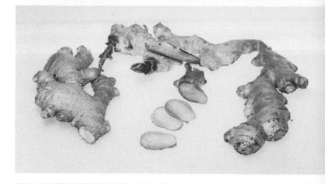

GINGER, SWEET MIXED: Also known as *sub gum geung* or *sub gum* vegetables, this is canned or jarred sweet and sour ginger mixed with vegetables. It can be used as a garnish or chilled and eaten as a relish. Use the juice in place of vinegar when making sweet and sour sauce and discover the taste difference.

GLUTINOUS RICE FLOUR: Flour milled from glutinous rice, an opaque, white, short and round rice that is very sticky when cooked. (*Naw mai.*)

HOISIN SAUCE: A deep brownish red sauce made from soy beans, chili, garlic and vinegar. Very thick, spicy and sweet, it's used in seasoning spareribs, roasting poultry and as a condiment, particularly with Peking Duck. (*Hoisin cheung.*)

JUJUBE NUT: See red dates, dried.

 **LEMON SAUCE:** A thick, jam like amber colored sauce made from lemon and sugar. We use this sauce to season ducks, or sometimes I spread a little over buttered toast or biscuits for a most unique and refreshing treat. (*Ning moan jeung.*)

 LICHEE: This fruit has a red, strawberry like skin with a white, translucent, juicy, sweet pulp. It's available in cans and is delicious when chilled.

 LILY BUDS, DRIED: The Chinese name is *gum jum.* A dried, 2 inch long flower, burnished gold in color. They must be soaked and knotted to keep from falling apart during cooking. The small, hard lump at the end of each stem should be removed. Lily buds add a delicate, subtle flavor to poultry and often are used in vegetarian dishes.

MUSHROOMS, DRIED CHINESE: These come in several grades with the best grade called *fa goo*. They are thick and light in color on the underside, while the surfaces of the caps have many cracks. The edges are curled. When purchased by weight, you can be sure every *fa goo* is almost uniform in size. *Fa goo* should be saved for special dishes in which mushrooms are cooked whole. For other uses, buy less expensive grades, since size uniformity is inconsequential when the recipe calls for slicing or dicing. They must be soaked until soft; the stems are discarded and the caps cut according to directions.

MUSTARD GREENS: A jade green vegetable with a thick stem and wide, curved leaves. It's slightly cool and bitter to the taste. Excellent for soup and a favorite pickling vegetable. (*Guy choy.*)

OYSTER SAUCE: A thick, rich, brown sauce made from oysters but without a strong, fishy odor. Its consistency is much like catsup. It's a favorite seasoning for meat but also is used as a condiment, especially with White Chop Chicken. (*Ho yow.*)

PICKLED MUSTARD: See turnips, Szechwan.

PLUM SAUCE: A thick, amber sauce with a pungent, spicy flavor, it's made from plums, apricots, vinegar and sugar. This chutney-like sauce is used as one of the condiments for Peking Duck and is also called duck sauce. It can be stored for months, refrigerated, in a tightly covered jar. (*Sheung moy cheung.*)

RED DATES, DRIED: Also known as *jujube* nuts, these are small, dried, red fruits with wrinkled, glossy skins. Used in soups or in steamed dishes to impart a subtle sweetness (*Hoan jo.*)

RICE NOODLES: A soft, white, flat noodle made from rice flour. It is about ½ inch wide. It can be made at home or purchased from Chinatown stores in pre cut strips or rolled in sheets. They can be stir fried or used like crepes in dim sum items. (*Fun.*)

 SALTED EGGS: Duck eggs which have been soaked in brine for 40 days. At the raw stage, the yolk hardens and turns a bright orange color; the white becomes cloudy, remains runny and will have a salty taste. You can cook it simply by boiling it as in making a hard boiled egg. Shell and cut in half. Delicious! (*Hom daan.*)

SAUSAGE, CHINESE: See Chinese Sausage.

 SESAME OIL: A seasoning oil with a nut like flavor. It's never used for cooking. A half teaspoon sprinkled on top will do wonders for any dish. (*Ma yau.*)

蝦米 **SHRIMP, DRIED:** Small, dried shrimps about ½ inch long. Should be soaked before using. They impart a very delicate and subtle flavor. (*Ha mai.*)

生抽豉油 **SOY SAUCE:** A thin, brown sauce made from soy beans, wheat, yeast and salt. There are two kinds: (1) Light or thin. Lighter in color and density, it's used as a condiment or in cooking dishes in which the color of the sauce shouldn't show, as in seafood. (2) Dark, thick or black. This soy sauce is darker, thicker and has a full bodied flavor. It's used when a deep brown color is desired. (*Sang chau, see yau.*)

八角 **STAR ANISE:** A small cluster of dark-brown, dry seeds shaped like an 8 pointed flower. It has a strong licorice flavor and is used in making soy sauce chicken, stewing beef and in some soups. (*Bot gok.*)

SWEET BEAN PASTE: A puree red bean paste used as a filling in many sweet Chinese pastries. (*Dow sa.*)

SWEET CUCUMBERS: See tea melons.

SWEET MIXED GINGER: See ginger, sweet mixed.

TAPIOCA STARCH: Sold by the pound in Chinese grocery stores, it is used as a sauce thickener and also in making certain types of wrappers in dim sum pastries. (*Ling fun.*)

TARO: The starchy root of a tropical plant. It is somewhat like potato but much more delicate. (*Wu tao.*)

TEA MELON: Also known as sweet cucumber. The Chinese name is *cha gwa*. Amber colored cucumber like squash preserved in a syrup of honey and spices. The tiny squash is only 2 to 3 inches long and is sweet in flavor and crunchy in texture. Use chopped melons as condiment for *joak*—the thick Chinese rice soup—or slice them to steam with pork dishes. The tea melons are available in cans. After it is opened, store in a jar and refrigerate. They will keep for months.

TOFU: See bean cake.

羅白 **TURNIP, CHINESE:** Known as *lo bak* in Chinese or *daikon* in Japanese. Daikon often is more readily available than lo bak. This white vegetable looks like an over-grown horseradish. It has a subtle flavor but exudes a very strong odor while cooking. Good for soups.

 冲菜 **TURNIP, SALTED:** Brown, with a salty flavor, these turnips can be used sparingly in meat dishes in place of salt. Adds flavor and textural interest. (*Choan choy.*)

炸菜 **TURNIP, SZECHWAN:** Also known as pickled mustard, this hot, peppery, canned turnip is preserved with Szechwan pepper. Use in steamed dishes and sour and hot soup. (*Ja choy.*)

馬蹄 **WATER CHESTNUTS:** A bulb like vegetable, the size of a strawberry, grown in water. The fresh ones are covered with mud and must be washed and peeled before eating. Yes, you can eat them raw. They're delicious! Crunchy and sweet, they're also available in cans. Good for stir frying when sliced or used in meat stuffings when minced. (*Ma tai.*)

 澄麵粉 **WHEAT STARCH:** Sold by the pound in Chinese grocery stores, they are used in making certain types of wrappers in dim sum pastries. (*Dung mein fun.*)

 雲吞皮 **WONTON WRAPPERS:** Made with flour, eggs and water, these can be purchased in Chinatown noodle factories or in some supermarket frozen food sections. Immediately rewrap unused portion with plastic wrap and freeze. (*Won ton pay.*)

INDEX OF RECIPES:

Steamed:

Chinese Pork Sausage Buns (*Lop Cheung Bow*), 44
Nine Layer Pudding Cake (*Gow Chung Go*), 65
Shrimp Boats (*Ha Yeung Dow Fu*), 42-44
Shrimp Bonnets (*Ha Gow*), 14-16
Steamed Barbecued Pork Buns (*Cha Siu Bow*), 18-19
Steamed Meat Dumplings (*Siu Mai*), 17-18
Steamed Pork Turnovers (*Fun Guaw*), 16-17
Steamed Rice Noodle Rolls (*Gee Cheung Fun*), 42
Steamed Sponge Cake (*Gai Don Go*), 60-
Stuffed Rice Noodle Rolls (*Guen Fun*), 20-21
Sweet Bean Paste Buns (*Dow San Bow*), 44
Sweet Rice Pudding Cake (*Bok Tong Go*), 22-23
Taro Pudding Cake (*Wu Tao Go*), 42
White Turnip Pudding Cake (*Lo Bok Go*), 66-68

Noodles:

Bean Sauce Noodles (*Ja Jeung Mein*), 55
Beef Chow Fun (*Gnow Yoke Chow Fun*), 49-50
Don Don Noodles (*Don Don Mein*), 52
Pork Lo Mein (*Gee Yoke Lo Mein*), 50-51

Tomato Beef Chowmein (*Fon Care Gnow Yoke Chow Mein*), 50
Yee Foo Wor Wonton (*Yee Foo Wonton*), 52-53

Miscellaneous:

Almond Float (*Hung Yun Lichee*), 61
Chinese Tamales (*Joan*), 70-71
Curried Chicken Wings (*Ga Lei Gai Yik*), 29
Egg Noodle Dough, 9
Glutinous Rice Dough, 11
Muu Shu Pork (*Mu Shu Yoke*), 39-40
Pickled Mustard Greens (*Suen Gai Choy*), 29
Rice Noodle Dough, 10-11
Steamed or Baked Bun Dough, 9-10
Sweet and Sour Sauce (*Teem Suen Jeung*), 14
Thick Rice Soup (*Joak*), 53
Wheat Starch Dough, 11

OTHER BOOKS BY TAYLOR & NG:

WOKCRAFT by Charles & Violet Schafer. An authoritative and entertaining book on the art of Chinese wok cookery. Authentic, easy to follow recipes for beginners and professionals alike. Illustrated by Win Ng.

RICECRAFT. Authoress Margaret Gin delves into the fact, fiction and fancy of rice. A collection of inventive recipes takes full advantage of the international versatility of rice. Fanciful illustrations by Win Ng.

TEACRAFT—a treasury of romance, rituals, and recipes. A book of tea—its multiplicity of uses and varieties, how to test and taste, plus recipes to complement teatime. Written by Charles & Violet Schafer, illustrated by Win Ng.

BREADCRAFT by Charles & Violet Schafer. A connoisseur's collection of bread recipes: what bread is, how you make it, and how you can create your own bread style. Plus a chapter devoted to breadspreads! Illustrated by Barney Wan.

PLANTCRAFT by Janet Cox. A practical and fun guide to indoor plant care. Illustrated charts depict the growing characteristics and conditions for over 60 plant varieties. Photo gallery by L. C. Spaulding Taylor.

HERBCRAFT by Violet Schafer. The mystery of herbs unveiled: 87 pages describe 26 herbs—their origin, history, use, growing and storing conditions. Illustrated by Win Ng.

COFFEE. The story behind your morning cup: Charles & Violet Schafer elaborate on coffee—its origin, many varieties, how to brew it and what to brew it in. With recipes for companion foods. Illustrations and photography by Alan Wood.

CHINESE VILLAGE COOKBOOK. Authoress Rhoda Yee tells her story—all about the wok and wok cookery, coupled with colorful narratives on everyday life in a Chinese village. A stir fry chart, photographic food glossary and authentic recipes guide the novice to wok mastery in no time!

DR. TERRI McGINNIS' DOG & CAT GOOD FOOD BOOK. Authoress Terri McGinnis, veterinarian and pet expert, unravels fact from fiction in this up to date, clear, concise, and convenient guide to pet nutrition: what to look for in commercial foods, how to cook up your own at home, how to recognize and feed special needs. Illustrated by Margaret Choi.